OUT OF SILENCE
The Woman's Guild
1887–1987

Mamie Magnusson

THE SAINT ANDREW PRESS
· EDINBURGH ·

First published in 1987 by
THE SAINT ANDREW PRESS
121 George Street, Edinburgh

Copyright © 1987 The Saint Andrew Press

ISBN 0 7152 0600 1

British Library Cataloguing in Publication Data
Magnusson, Mamie
Out of silence: the Woman's Guild
1887–1987.
1. Church of Scotland. *Woman's Guild*
History
I. Title
267'.4452411   BX9075.A2C5

ISBN 0-7152-0600-1

Photoset in Great Britain by
Rowland Phototypesetting Ltd, Bury St Edmunds, Suffolk
and printed by St Edmundsbury Press Ltd
Bury St Edmunds, Suffolk

Contents

Foreword

For years I have felt that there was a tale to be told about the birth and growth of the Woman's Guild. So on hearing that The Saint Andrew Press were prepared to publish a book for the Guild's Centenary, I was delighted. However, there was within the Guild some apprehension that the author might write in the condescending manner all too familiar to most women's organisations, or might fail to get the true 'feel' of the Guild. Mamie Magnusson's book dispels these fears. Her easy style, her painstaking research, her obvious ability to listen to people, the fascinating asides on the changing social attitudes and prejudices so characteristic of this period, all combine to make the book a very good and interesting read indeed.

Dr Charteris founded the Woman's Guild to organise the work in which women were engaged and to enrich their spiritual lives. In its approach to the Centenary, the Guild has been rethinking, for the late 1980s and beyond, the Aim of its members—'to dedicate their lives to the Lord Jesus Christ through Worship, Fellowship and Service'. Although the times and social mores differ from those of 1887, the need is just as great for the voices of Christian women to be heard, and their service offered in the name of Christ. To survive, the Guild must enter its second century regarding it as an opportunity for challenge and renewal. And since much can be learned from the past, a special conference is planned.

Mrs Magnusson refers to the Guild as 'a great family of women' which she 'cannot ever imagine coming to an end'. Nevertheless, Guild membership, like that of the Church as a whole, has been decreasing over a number of years, and people have been forecasting the Guild's demise for almost as long as I can remember! I find it equally hard to think of the Guild coming to an end when I travel around the country meeting enthusiastic and dedicated women of all ages giving much time and energy to work for their Church and their Guild. But, no organisation can rest on past achievements. The Guild never has and must not do so now. Much of the pioneering work referred to in this book has gradually been taken over by the Church as a whole, and new interests and avenues of service constantly come into focus. These include representing the Guild on the Women's National Commission which brings to our attention matters of current legislation and social concern.

A welcome feature of recent years has been a growing involvement, especially at national level, with churchwomen from overseas. Contact has been made with Woman's Guilds from several African countries as well as with Bermuda. An exchange visit with East German church-women has taken place; and I think Dr Charteris would have been interested to see the Guild National President at a conference in Helsinki of churchwomen from both Eastern and Western Europe discussing nuclear energy and world peace, resulting in letters going to heads of Churches and Governments! Women have come a long way in the past 100 years and it is good to look back in gratitude for the firm foundation upon which so many Scottish women have been able confidently to build.

This has been a memorable time not only for myself but for the dedicated team of Vice-Presidents and staff and for all members of committees who have worked so hard for the Centenary nationally and locally. I have heard from all over the country heart-warming reports of imaginative schemes involving service and gifts to Church and community, and many acts of rededication, in addition to 'Guild Sunday' services and a BBC 'Songs of Praise' programme from Glasgow Cathedral. Central Committee has chosen the new Guild Hymn and has resolved to urge Branches and Young Woman's Groups to undertake some special new piece of service and to make real efforts to bring Branches and Groups more closely together in this and other ways.

We have been most grateful for the generous help which has been forthcoming from such organisations as the Post Office, who are printing a special Woman's Guild Centenary slogan on all mail posted in Edinburgh during a week of our choice; from local authorities; and from several other commercial and industrial concerns. The Guild is held in high regard!

At the close of my Report on the Guild, the General Assembly of 1986 agreed to mark the Guild Centenary by some special event at the 1987 Assembly. The Guild Annual Meeting in April 1987 promises a day of great thanksgiving, looking to the past but also to the future. The Guild will be entering the 1987–88 session with the Annual Theme: 'Praise for the Past—Hope for the Future'.

The Guild owes a great debt of gratitude to The Saint Andrew Press and to Mrs Mamie Magnusson for recording the story of so many women of the Church of Scotland and their emergence 'Out of Silence'.

May Smith (National President 1984–87)

Acknowledgments

Writing the history of the Woman's Guild has been an immensely rewarding task, for it has given me the opportunity of getting to know a huge new family; my only regret is that so many of them have no individual mention in these pages—the unsung thousands of women who have served the Guild so loyally down the years, the generations of local presidents and secretaries, treasurers, deputies, delegates, editors, members of committees and sub-committees, study groups and working parties. All these, and the countless thousands of ordinary Guild members, are the backbone of the organisation, and it is to them that this book is dedicated.

I wrote to *Life and Work* in October 1985 asking Guildswomen everywhere to send me their memories, and how well they responded! I received scores of replies, many of them from very old ladies, full of wisdom and humour and a keen perception of the fun and fellowship of being a Guildswoman. It would have been impossible to use them all individually, alas; but there were a few excerpts that I could not resist using, and each and every letter helped to give me some of the rich flavour of what it means, and meant, to be part of the Guild. I was sent cherished photographs, letters, diaries, books, brochures, long-service certificates and other memorabilia. In particular, Mr James Anderson, Session Clerk of Moffat-linked-with-Wamphray, was a mine of information about the founder's birthplace and lent me his precious copy of the history of Wamphray; and the last president of Wamphray Guild, Mrs Burnet, gave me good Guild hospitality and guided me to Mrs J A M Carlyle, who generously let me have her own immaculate research on the history of Wamphray and her copy of the 1841 *Statistical Account*.

The Woman's Guild headquarters staff in Edinburgh gave me access to all their records, and were unfailingly helpful and courteous every time I knocked on their door. I am especially grateful to Mrs Kathleen Beveridge who started me off on my research before she retired as secretary, and her successor, Mrs Lorna Paterson, who bore with me cheerfully in the midst of managing all the centenary celebrations. Others to whom I owe warm thanks are Mr Bob Kernohan, Editor of *Life and Work*; Miss Elma Sloan, DCS, and Miss Kay Ramsay, DCS, of the Board of World Mission and Unity; Mrs Kathleen Anderson, whose careful chronicle of Guild events, culled from 90 years of *Blue Books*, provided an invaluable chronological framework; and to every surviving Guild president, who all patiently helped me to gain an understanding of Guild policies and Church committees. In addition, Mrs Mary Millican (President, 1975–78) read and checked the completed manuscript.

Many books provided background material; but by far the most important was the splendid *Life of Archibald Hamilton Charteris*, by the Honourable Arthur Gordon, which I plundered shamelessly in trying to recapture something of the remarkable character of the man who founded the Woman's Guild.

The Woman's Guild is above all a family, and my own family were a tremendous source of inspiration and help: especially my daughter, Anna Magnusson, who did a great deal of research and compiled the Index, my husband, Magnus Magnusson, who insisted on checking and re-typing the whole manuscript—and enjoyed it hugely; and my sister, Anna Baird, who kept the family alive during my unforgettable year with the Woman's Guild.

Mamie Magnusson

I

The Boy from Wamphray

The little boy sitting at the end of one of the benches in the crowded schoolroom in the village of Wamphray was barely two years old. He clutched his slate pencil with awkward infant fingers and bit the end of his tongue in fierce concentration as he tried to copy the letters on the blackboard. When the older boys and girls recited their catechisms, his trailing treble could be heard at the end of every phrase. Sometimes he would wander over to the large Bible in the corner of the room, and one of the big boys, waiting for the teacher to hear his Latin verbs, would help the wee boy to turn the pages; he would guide the small finger through the parable that had been the morning Bible reading, and point out the difficult words written up on the blackboard. Then 'Wee Erchie', as he was known to the pupils of Wamphray Parish School, would suddenly lose interest, toddle quietly across to the door that connected the schoolroom with the schoolhouse, reach up and open it with both hands, slip through and shut the door silently behind him. The class could just hear him, if it happened to be a quiet moment, calling for his mammy to give him a jam piece before he went back 'to play'.

For this was no infant prodigy escaping from the tyranny of a too-early education. This was Archie Charteris, son of the school-master of Wamphray, a little Borders village in Upper Annandale, Dumfriesshire. The schoolhouse was his home. The schoolroom was his playground, a magic world of children of all ages cosily crammed into one room: children reading, singing, reciting, drawing, measuring, making things, doing things. 'Wee Erchie' came in and out of the schoolroom as he pleased from the day he could walk, and he joined in whatever gave him pleasure. It was fun to sing and recite and listen to the stories from the reading-books. He loved the smell of chalk and ink, and the sound of squeaking pencils on slate, and the organised bustle of 120 children aged from 6 to 16 or more, some learning the alphabet, some doing algebra, some reciting Homer—all studying under one teacher, 'the maister', Archie's father, John Charteris.

It was this one-roomed, low-roofed school, and the schoolhouse next door (as well as what had happened, what was happening, and what was about to happen in a Scottish village so small that it is hard to find on any map) that turned young Archie Charteris into the great man he was to become: not just the Professor of Biblical Criticism at the University of Edinburgh; not just Moderator of the General Assembly of the Church of Scotland, and Chaplain to Queen Victoria and King Edward VII; not just the man who brought new life and inspiration to a Church riven by decades of disruption; but the man who brought thousands of women out of silence and founded the biggest organisation of women that Scotland has ever known—the Woman's Guild.

Everything stemmed from Wamphray School, which was to be taken over as a smiddy when a new school was built in 1860, and is now a private dwelling. It was made up of two ordinary cottages built end to end, with a small extension added later for boarders. Archie was born (as were his younger brother Matthew and sister Mary) in the box-bed at the back of the schoolhouse. The date was 13 December 1835, two years before Victoria became Queen. The schoolmaster's baby was christened Archibald Hamilton Charteris in the school itself, which was being used for church services while Wamphray Parish Church was being rebuilt—not before time, it would seem, because the minister, the Revd Charles Dickson, had written of the old church in the previous year for the *New Statistical Account of Scotland*: 'Altogether, it is damp, dirty, and disagreeable both in summer and winter—by far the worst place of worship in the south of Scotland'.[1] Rebuilding must have started immediately, because the 150th Anniversary of the new Wamphray Parish Church was celebrated in October 1984.

Apart from his early entry into the school, there was little anyone could remember about the young Archie Charteris that would have singled him out for greatness. True, he was able to read from the New Testament to his dying grandfather at the age of three. He could read a French fable at five, and had started on Gibbon's *Decline and Fall of the Roman Empire* when he was eight. But he himself always put this kind of thing down as 'bits and pieces' picked up parrot-fashion in his 'playing' days in the schoolroom. He was rather small as a boy, not shy but sensitive, with a slight hesitation in his speech which turned out to be a help rather than a hindrance when he became a preacher. He could be a grave little lad for his years, but he was also full of life, a healthy active boy running around barefoot in the summer, keen on football and swimming; and like every true Borders boy, he could ride a horse.

The games the boys played in Wamphray Glen among the wooded slopes beside the Wamphray Water re-enacted the deeds of their forebears, the 'brave Wamphray lads' of ballad fame, the Border reivers whose sport and livelihood it was to go on regular sheep-stealing raids into England, and who just as regularly saw their own houses plundered and their livestock carried off by the English. During history lessons in the schoolroom the children learned how one of their ancestors, John Johnstone of Howgill, was called to a court at Castlemilk, near Glasgow, in 1569, after the defeat of Mary Queen of Scots at Langside, and had to promise Regent Murray to guarantee 'the good behaviour of the auld gang of Wamphray'. The children liked to hear, too, how Bonnie Prince Charlie's Highlanders had come through Wamphray in 1745 and stopped to salute the funeral cortège of a former minister of Wamphray, the Revd Taylor, who had been deposed by the General Assembly in 1718 for removing the march-stones round the glebe. When the mourners came out of the kirkyard, they found that the Highlanders had stolen their best horses.

Common ancestry linked all the pupils in the school. Everyone had some connection with everyone else. Cousins shared benches with half-cousins and young uncles with nephews. A person who did not belong to Wamphray either by birth or marriage was a rarity in the parish before the coming of the Caledonian Railway, which Archie Charteris watched being laid when he was a schoolboy. Today, the rail link that took him to university and renown is no more, and Wamphray has settled back into peaceful rural obscurity among the hills, reached only by a country road from the busy A74, between Beattock and Lockerbie.

The Charteris family could trace their lineage back to Sir John Charteris of Amisfield, whose family intermarried with the Maxwells and Douglases of Drumlanrig; but Archie Charteris never talked of such things, always remembering his father's motto: 'If you don't add further lustre to your name and pedigree, don't mention either'. But Archie loved to tell that his maternal grandfather and namesake, Archibald Hamilton from Torthorwald, had ridden 'knee to knee' with Robert Burns in the Dumfries Yeomanry, and that grandfather Hamilton's younger brother James was one of the squad of yeomanry who fired a salute over the poet's grave at his burial in St Michael's churchyard, Dumfries, in 1796.

Archie's mother belonged to a famous Covenanting family, the Hamiltons of Preston; and to understand Charteris the man, who was to make such a mark on Scotland's religious history, one has to remember the strong streak of convenanting blood in his veins and also little Wamphray's own part in that bitter struggle for civil and religious liberty led by the signatories of the Scottish National Covenant of 1638. The Revd John Brown, minister of Wamphray from 1655, was outlawed by Acts of Parliament in 1662 for calling his brethren of the presbytery 'perjured knaves and villains' because they attended the Episcopal Diocesan Synod of Glasgow. He was banished to Holland, where he died 17 years later. Another Wamphray minister (1690–95), the Revd Thomas Douglas, had already had a swashbuckling career as a Covenanter before he came to Wamphray; he had ridden into Rutherglen with Robert Hamilton of Preston on 29 May 1679, with 80 armed men, and had burned there, at the Mercat Cross, all the Acts of the Scottish Parliament opposed to civil and religious liberty. Three days later, his sermon at the Drumclog Conventicle had been interrupted by the dragoons of Claverhouse—which led to their celebrated defeat at the Battle of Drumclog. Mr Douglas was outlawed by the government and had a price put on his head; but he survived, and spent the last five years of his life preaching in peace at Wamphray.

Such were the tales and the stirring history that Archie Charteris fed upon during his childhood in Wamphray, and he grew up with a strong sense of national identity and a love of things Scottish that was to influence the important decisions he was to make in later life. But his was not the chip-on-the-shoulder Scottishness, the in-bred bitterness and sense of inferiority, that can lead to narrow parochialism. Rather, he was an internationalist, so secure in his own roots that he was not afraid to experiment with ideas that were foreign to Scotland. He went round churches and missions throughout England, France, Germany and the Low Countries before formulating his great plan for the women of the Church of Scotland; and there is no doubt that his lack of narrowness was largely due to the breadth of the education he received from his father at Wamphray Parish School.

It was exactly the same education open to every other child in Wamphray under a statute of the Scottish Parliament in 1696, compelling the chief landowners, or heritors, in every parish to provide a school and a salary for the teacher. It was an education second to none anywhere in the world at that time. In that little school in a remote Scottish glen, the sons and daughters of the poorest ploughman, the richest farmer, the minister, the schoolmaster and the tinker, all sat side by side learning Latin and Greek, French, German and mathematics, receiving the finest of groundings in the three Rs; and all rooted and fixed in a strong, uncompromising base of religious instruction.

There was tremendous disparity in the kind of money earned by the parishioners of Wamphray. The minister himself was relatively comfortably off; the Revd Charles Dickson's stipend as a minister of the established Church of Scotland was a handsome £253 13s 4d a year, 'exclusive of £8 6s 8d for communion elements'. He had a 'commodious and comfortable' manse, and a glebe ('supposed to be about eight or nine Scotch acres') which brought him in another £12 a year.

By contrast, Mr Charteris the schoolmaster only earned £7 a year when he first went to Wamphray. It should have been £23 a year, but his predecessor's retirement pension of £16 was deducted from the new teacher's salary. In 1834 the statutory allowance was raised from £23 to £34; but the additional £11 did not all go to Mr Charteris: £4 went to the pensioner, and only £7 to the teacher. So Mr Charteris only received £14 in the end, instead of the full £34; and it was not until the old man died in 1839 that Mr Charteris finally got his statutory pay of £34 a year. In addition he received pupils' fees of around £25 a year, paid either by parents or with the help of the kirk session. He had a house and garden, and he boarded children from outlying districts. He was an elder of the parish kirk, session clerk, and Inspector of the Poor.

Farm labourers at that time were earning 1/6 to 1/8 a day in summer, and 1/2 a day in winter; masons, carpenters and slaters got 2/6 a day in summer and 2/- in winter, 'without victuals'. Men-servants were paid from five to seven guineas a half-year, 'with victuals', and maid-servants got £2 to £3 a half-year, 'with victuals'.

Below even this subsistence level, there was an average of 12 people out of the parish population of 600 who were receiving aid from parish funds in 1834. They had their rent and repairs paid for them, and were supplied with potatoes and peat, and between six and eight shillings in cash every three months.

'They are in general kept tolerably comfortable,' reported the Revd Charles Dickson, 'and none of them have occasion to beg.' He noted 'a disposition among the poor to refrain from seeking parochial relief, which they consider as degrading'. Most families were linked by marriage or ancestry, and on the whole those who were better-off looked after their poorer relations. In fact, wrote the Revd Dickson, 'great swarms of beggars who flock from other quarters, frequently from Ireland . . . extort far more from the inhabitants in the course of the year, than our own poor derive from all the sources.'

School attendance was not compulsory; and when Archie Charteris moved to Edinburgh and then Glasgow, he saw for the first time children deprived of their educational birthright, orphaned waifs who had never seen the inside of a schoolroom, children abandoned to fend for themselves in the desperate conditions that the Industrial Revolution brought to Scotland's cities and large towns. The Scots' veneration for learning was seen to best advantage in the country parish, where every child was known and counted, and the kirk session kept a firm fatherly eye on all of its flock. There was many a village school in Scotland which, like Wamphray with its population of just under 600 in 1834, sent a regular stream of students straight to university and often to high academic renown. There were many other country parishes which could boast, as the Revd Charles Dickson did in the *New Statistical Account*: 'There are none, old or young, but can read, and few that cannot write'. But what was special about Wamphray was the calibre of its schoolmaster from 1823 to 1871—John Charteris.

In his own day, after a basic elementary education at Wamphray, John Charteris had had to go to Applegarth school to study classics, modern languages and mathematics under a university graduate. Then he came back to his home parish to pass on what he had learned to generations of Wamphray children. His son, Professor Archibald Charteris, was later to describe that education as follows:

> Before we left school [around 14 years of age] we had read as much Latin and Greek and Mathematics as made it easy for us to pass the junior and enter the second class at the University. . . . We could have passed any ordinary examination in Virgil, Livy, and Horace in Latin; on Homer, Anacreon, and several plays of Euripides in Greek. With Euclid we were quite familiarly acquainted, and with Algebra up to the Binomial Theorem. French we could read easily. All the clever girls learned it also. . . . We read German fairly well. We went through a course of Navigation. We were taught to measure fields and draw plans of the farm we measured. One of us, having been thoroughly grounded in Mensuration in this way, but with no other training, became the able surveyor of the land of a wide and populous British colony.[2]

During his 48 years as 'maister' of Wamphray, John Charteris turned out ten ministers, including three who rose to the highest position in the Church of Scotland—Moderator of the General Assembly. All three of them had sat on his school benches at the same time: his son Archie (Moderator 1892), John Pagan, minister of Forgandenny and Bothwell (1899), and John Gillespie, of Mouswald, author of *Humours of Scottish Life* (Moderator in 1903). Nineteen pupils of John Charteris became doctors. One of them was his younger son, Matthew, who was Professor of Materia Medica and Therapeutics at the University of Glasgow from 1880 to 1897. Eleven became teachers and headmasters of schools in Scotland and abroad. There were also surveyors, merchants, an army general, a song-writer, master-craftsmen, tradesmen and a host of successful businessmen.

John Charteris gave the higher education to every child able and willing to take it (Archie joined the Latin class at the age of six), while attending to 120 pupils of all ages assembled in the one room. Several classes were going on at the same time, from the six-year-olds learning their alphabet to the young farmer who had been persuaded to come back and catch up on missed schooling. Older pupils helped to teach the younger, and Professor Charteris was later to write:

> Some educational theorists say that to have advanced pupils prevents a master from attending to beginners and young children. . . . I have seen many schools, and I have never seen one where the average pupil made quicker progress, or where the dull child was more stimulated and helped to do his best, than in Wamphray school when I was a pupil.

It all called for tremendous teamwork and organisation, and these were the two things above all that characterised Archie Charteris' life's work. He believed in teamwork, and he was a brilliant organiser. Organisation was the whole theme of his beloved Woman's Guild. In actual fact, he did not found a Guild—he founded 'The Organisation of Woman's Work'.

Notes to Chapter 1

1 *New Statistical Account of Scotland*, by the Ministers of the Respective Parishes, under the Superintendence of a Committee of the Society for the Benefit of the Sons and Daughters of the Clergy (William Blackwood: Dumfriesshire, 1841), p 146
2 Arthur Gordon, *The Life of Archibald Hamilton Charteris* (Hodder & Stoughton, 1913), pp 11–12

2

Woman's Work

Woman's work in Wamphray was much the same as woman's work anywhere else in Scotland in the first half of the nineteenth century: at best comfortably domestic, at worst distressingly menial. A woman of means (and that meant a woman whose husband or other male guardian had means) spent her days organising other women to do the cooking and cleaning for her household, care for her children and nurse her babies; other women did all these things for the rich until their own marriage, when they did them for themselves. In the rapidly growing towns and cities, women did hard labour in the most lowly tasks in factories and mills, at only half the wages paid to men for the same job. In the pits, women carried coal on their backs.

Girls went straight from village school at the age of 12 or 13 into domestic service in the big country houses. Girls from the big houses would either be taught at home by governesses, or else sent to small private schools and seminaries for young ladies in the cities. But whatever their education, it made little difference to their 'career' prospects: apart from a very few private teaching posts, there were no openings for educated women in business or commerce. Nursing was unskilled, unorganised and insanitary, and would remain so until 1856 at least, when Florence Nightingale returned from the Crimean War to start her campaign to lift nursing towards the dignity of a proper profession for women. All other professions were closed to them. It was 1886 before women were allowed to train and practise as doctors in Scotland, and 1889 before an Act was passed allowing women to graduate at Scottish universities—although as a matter of fact women had already been studying some subjects at Scottish universities for years, thanks to enlightened lecturers like Professor Archibald Charteris who held a ladies' class in Biblical Criticism at Edinburgh in the 1870s.

Charteris' sympathy for the cause of higher education for women was inherited from his father, whose schoolroom at Wamphray was distinguished not only by the size of its Latin, Greek, French and German groups but also by the presence of girls in those groups. John Charteris was many years ahead, even of Scotland's superior education standards, in providing tuition up to university entrance standards for any Wamphray girl able and willing to absorb it, even if her career prospects were limited to kindling fires and emptying chamber pots at the laird's house before early marriage to a ten-shillings-a-week ploughman. It was to be 1906—35 years after John Charteris died —before the list of former Wamphray pupils who were studying at universities or colleges would include a woman: Miss Winifred Wight, an art student at a college in Kensington, and daughter of the Revd George Wight, minister at Wamphray for over 50 years.

John Charteris could teach the girls; but he could do nothing to remove the prejudices, traditions and social conditions that regulated what women could or could not do. For instance, he started a debating society, known as the 'Gabbing School', to encourage his school-leavers to be articulate and keep up with public affairs; but it was for young men only. Women were neither admitted to membership nor allowed to attend meetings as observers. There was nothing unusual in that: women were not expected to mix socially on equal terms with men, nor were they expected to voice opinions of their own in public. Wamphray folk long remembered the temerity of a lady who stood up at a meeting convened for secular matters concerning the Church and began to speak her mind on the subject under discussion; whereupon the chairman, an old elder, with head erect, called out in a commanding voice, 'Seelence there!' She sat down at once, although reports say that she was 'mumbling something' (probably 'Silly old goat'!).[1]

It is also reported that in 1835, when a methodist preacher and his wife, who were on a missionary tour, came to Wamphray and held an open-air service under an oak-tree near the village, the whole country-side turned out—not to hear him, but because it had been advertised that his wife would preach too. More than half a century later, Professor Archibald Charteris would be trying to persuade the women of Scotland to speak up and speak out in their new role as Guilds-women; and nearly 150 years later, it is still one of the most difficult jobs of Guild leaders to get women to accept any office that involves speaking in public. Maybe it is these generations of 'Seelence there!' that are to blame. Perhaps things might have been different if the Wam-phray girls had been allowed to join the 'Gabbing School'. But at least they did have one concession: whether with the schoolmaster's knowl-edge or not (and I rather suspect that it was), the owner of the house in

which the debates were held would allow the girls to climb up into the
loft and sit there out of sight, listening to the weighty discussions of the
men and boys.

It all seems humiliating to us in these days of so-called sex equality,
but this was the way things had always been. Most women accepted
their place in society. Those with the means to be free of domestic
chores would spend their time at the easel or the piano, visiting,
dressing up, going to social events, and talking a lot—but in private
(perhaps all the allegedly idle gossip of which women are accused was
simply compensation for all those years of enforced 'seelence' in
public). Other women of substance would give themselves over to
'good works', visiting the sick, taking food and clothing to the poor,
and collecting for charities. Lady Grisell Baillie, whom Charteris was to
choose as the first deaconess of the Church of Scotland and the leading
light of the Woman's Guild, was one of those Victorian women of
noble birth whose days were dedicated to religious works, constant
prayer and 'visitations' to the sick and needy. Her life, according to
Charteris, was 'a revelation of happy saintliness'.

His own mother's lot, as a farmer's daughter and a schoolmaster's
wife, is described in glowing terms in the biography of Professor
Charteris by the Revd, the Honourable Arthur Gordon. It is a portrait
of the ideal mother as seen through the eyes of a churchman at a time
when religion was still the most powerful influence in most people's
lives. In the quaint, pedantic language of the times, laced with Biblical
quotations, Mr Arthur Gordon gives a warm and revealing picture of a
good Scotswoman of a century ago, a woman somewhere in the middle
of the rigid class structure that was an accepted part of life:

> Called, by her own mother's death, early to play an eldest daughter's part
> in her father's household, superintend servants, cook food, and attend to
> thorough cleanliness in matters of dairy work and produce, she acquired,
> and she plainly required, the qualities of the virtuous woman who
> 'looketh well to the ways of her household, and eateth not the bread of
> idleness'. She was pre-eminently what is called a good manager, perhaps
> the greater power in guiding the family. She added prudence and
> reticence to her faculty of decision; was above mixing in parochial gossip
> or taking part in passing squabbles, could laugh quietly at the funny side
> of storms in a tea-cup. . . . But she was not a wife and mother merely
> providing for physical needs: she first impressed on her son's young
> mind the saving truths of religion and the meaning of the Church of God.
> The greater part of her reading was about the Church and its ministers;
> and the gist of her serious conversation, if it did not begin, generally
> ended on that subject. It was the joy and glory of his mother's life that her
> son should be a minister and leader in the Kingdom of Jesus Christ.[2]

Mrs Charteris also introduced her son to the world of Missions. When he was only six, young Archie walked with his mother the seven miles to Moffat and back, to hear the great Dr Alexander Duff, the Church of Scotland's first foreign missionary, appealing for funds for his work of conversion, care and education of the heathen in India. Although the Kirk did not send out its first official missionary until 1829, Scots missionaries had been going abroad for many years at their own expense or supported by various independent societies: David Livingstone, for instance, was sent to Africa by the London Missionary Society. Scottish congregations had been helping missions individually since at least the 1760s, when the General Assembly authorised a collection (it raised over £540) for the Scottish Society for the Propagation of Christian Knowledge among Red Indians. As early as 1775, Wamphray Church had collected 14 shillings to send to America to help establish a Scottish congregation in New Jersey.

Right from the outset, women were deeply involved in the foreign mission movement; indeed this was one area where they were not only on equal terms with men, but often far ahead of men in terms of enthusiasm and activity. The earliest missionaries often took their wives or sisters with them, and these pioneering women founded the first schools for women and girls in India. In 1819, the Calcutta Female Juvenile Society for the Education of Native Females was started by young Indian women who had been taught by the wives of Baptist missionaries in Calcutta. In 1822, a certain Miss Cook began a school for girls in Calcutta, and other missionaries' wives ran schools in Bombay. No fewer than six schools were started by the Aberdeen-educated wife of Dr John Wilson, from Lauder in Berwickshire, who ministered in India from 1828, first under the Scottish Missionary Society and then supported by the Church of Scotland. It was he who founded the renowned Wilson College in Bombay.

But every church and missionary society still baulked at the idea of commissioning *unmarried* women to go out as missionaries in their own right—or even of involving them in the organisation at home. As far back as 1797 a woman was complaining in an article in the *Missionary Magazine* about male dominance:

> Why are females alone excluded from all ostensible share in these labours of love? It cannot be denied, that some among them possess both ability and inclination suited to the purpose. Nor let it be argued that their own familiar and domestic concerns afford the only sphere of their exertions. Here, indeed, they ought undoubtedly to begin, but they are not called to stop there, when circumstances allow them to do otherwise. The common accounts of receipt and expenditure, together with minutes of

proceedings, *etc*, might, I think, be easily accomplished by females in the middle classes of life.[3]

Indeed they might; and in 1838 the first Scottish Women's Missionary Association (founded in 1837) appointed their first woman missionary, a Miss Reid, who unfortunately died within a year of her arrival in Bombay. Her successor, a Swiss woman, succumbed to cholera almost before she had begun her work. Dr John Wilson's sister-in-law, Miss Anna Bayne, who had gone to India as a voluntary helper entirely at her own expense, also died after four years' residence in Bombay. Not surprisingly, doubts began to be raised about whether women were physically tough enough to stand up to the rigours of the mission field. But worse was to come: in 1842 the Ladies' Committee in Edinburgh sent out a young woman missionary to Poona, on the strong recommendation of a young male missionary working there for the Church of Scotland—and within a year, the two were engaged to be married. The Ladies' Committee, in fury, thought of demanding compensation from the General Assembly's Foreign Missions Committee for filching its newly appointed woman missionary (who would now have to work alongside her husband); but it was reported that the Assembly's Committee might bring an action for damages 'for sending out Ladies so attractive as to draw off' men missionaries from their work. It was suggested that the Ladies' Committee should send out only middle-aged women (rather than young nubile ones) or married couples. The Ladies' Committee stuck to their guns, however, and continued to send out single women despite the double hazards of disease and romance.

Women's committees were formed all over Scotland to raise funds for the missionary societies or to send missionaries of their own. Edinburgh concentrated on the Indian sub-continent. Glasgow Ladies favoured Africa, and sent their first lady missionary to the Cape in 1842. As the British Empire expanded throughout the nineteenth century, missionary fervour increased, and Scotswomen were to be found teaching, nursing and doctoring all over India, in Africa, China and the West Indies, and among oppressed Jews in Turkey and Hungary, Greece, Lebanon, Egypt and the Holy Land; there, the Tabeetha Mission School was to become, like the Kalimpong Mission in India, the special pride and care of the Woman's Guild.

These brave women sometimes worked alongside the men on established mission stations; but frequently they operated alone, facing all kinds of danger, disease and deprivation, and dutifully sending regular reports home to the church or society that was supporting them. Mary Slessor, a mill-girl from Dundee, who was sent to Eastern

Nigeria in 1876 by the United Presbyterian Church, lived in a mud hut with a tribe which, when their chief died, buried alongside him four wives, eight slave men, eight slave women, and twenty girls and boys; when she died in 1915 there were nearly fifty churches and schools in the area. The Free Church Association sent Dr Jane Waterston from Inverness to be the first woman medical missionary in South Africa. The father of Dr Agnes Henderson, in Aberdeen, paid her full salary as a medical missionary in Nagpur in the central province of India; with the help of a second doctor, Dr Jenny Macphail, and a nurse, Miss Steen, she opened the splendidly-equipped Mure Memorial Hospital in 1896, which had been funded by two generous sisters in Ayrshire, the Misses Mure. Janet Beck served for 30 years in Livingstone, in Africa, entirely supported by her two sisters in Edinburgh. The Honourable Mary Scott, daughter of the 8th Lord Polwarth, served for 48 years in the Himalayas, without any salary. Women managed to breach the hitherto impregnable doors of the *zenana* (a kind of Indian harem), in which the women and girls of the household were kept locked away from the outside world. By 1875, women mission workers were running schools in 60 *zenanas* in Bengal, and all over Scotland women formed work-parties to raise funds for the Zenana Mission.

Yet when these early women missionaries came home on furlough, yellowed by sun and malaria, they had to sit demurely silent on platforms around the country while their male colleagues did all the talking about life in the mission field. The Methodist missionary's wife who had preached at the open-air service at Wamphray back in 1835 had been an exception, a phenomenon indeed. The idea of women speaking in public was so alien that even the trend-setting women of the Ladies' Missionary Association in Edinburgh never dreamed of holding a meeting without men in charge. Their original committee was composed of fifteen ladies and seven presidents—all men! So when, in 1875, they wanted a missionary to address meetings around Scotland on behalf of the Ladies' Association, they naturally appointed a man—the Revd William Ferguson from the Punjab; but he brought along a Miss Pigot, who was the Church of Scotland's pioneer worker in the *zenanas*, and suggested that she should talk about her work too. She was such a success that she ended up addressing no fewer than 42 meetings! Mr Ferguson's wife was promptly appointed the Association's chief speaker in her husband's place, and in the following year, 1876, when the ladies held their first conference during the annual meeting of the General Assembly of the Church of Scotland, *no men were present* —except, as a courtesy, Mr Ferguson, who presided 'by invitation', as the Minutes were careful to point out.

It was a small advance. As the novelist Annie S Swan was to write of those first women organisers:

> 'Criticism continued to be their portion from many quarters, for though, in comparison with the lot of their poor dark sisters abroad, they lived in Utopia, they were still hedged about by that deep ingrained conception of woman as a frail creature, inferior in every sense to man, to be cared for and protected by him—but, nevertheless, kept strictly in her proper place.'[4]

Archibald Hamilton Charteris would grow up to have very different ideas about women, and a determination to give them, for the first time, a real place in the affairs of the Church. That determination had its roots in a cataclysmic event that happened when he was only seven years old, and which tore Scotland apart—the Great Disruption.

Notes to Chapter 2

1 John Paterson, *Wamphray: Pages from the History and Traditions of a Famous Parish in Upper Annandale* (Lockerbie, 1900), p 184
2 Arthur Gordon, *The Life of Archibald Hamilton Charteris* (Hodder & Stoughton, 1913), pp 14–15
3 Elizabeth Hewat, *Vision and Achievement 1796–1956* (Nelson, 1960), p 11
4 Annie S Swan, *Seed Time and Harvest* (Nelson, 1937), p 69

3

'By Schisms Rent Asunder . . .'

There had been two churches in Wamphray when Archie Charteris was born. One was Wamphray Parish Church of Scotland, the established national Church of the land. The other was Gateside Relief Church, whose members had broken away from the national Church in the 1770s, along with many others all over Scotland, and formed their own Kirk 'for *relief* of Christians oppressed in their Christian privileges'. The particular privilege that they felt most oppressed in had been the long-cherished right of Scottish Presbyterians to choose their own minister. John Knox himself had laid down this right in his *First Book of Discipline*; but it had been eroded when Scotland and England were united under a UK Parliament in 1707. As the Established Church of Scotland, the Kirk came under the laws of the government in London; and the law that hurt most was the Law of Patronage, whereby the landlord was empowered to impose a minister on any parish on his land, whether the congregation wanted that particular choice or not. The 'Reliefers', as they were called, were not the first to secede from the Established Church over the principle of patronage; nor would they be the last.

Indeed, by the time Archie Charteris was eight years old the village of Wamphray had a *third* church: the Free Church, which was wrested from the mother Kirk in the great Disruption of 1843, when the Church of Scotland lost more than 450 of its 1200 ministers and 40 per cent of all its active members. Once again, the major cause of the exodus was a protest against patronage; but this time the effect was cataclysmic. The Kirk lost many of its most energetic leaders and much of its income, and all but one of its foreign missionaries—including its beloved pioneer in India, Dr Alexander Duff. Manses lay deserted, empty churches fell into disrepair and decay; depleted congregations had neither the heart nor the means—nor even a minister, often as not—to cope with the problem of the unchurched masses in the cities. The new Free Church

flourished, building fine churches, schools, colleges, and even a handsome Assembly Hall on the Mound in Edinburgh; but meanwhile the
old Kirk found itself in dire straits, demoralised and weakened on all
fronts.

Archie Charteris was not to learn the full effects of the Disruption
until he went to university in Edinburgh to study for the ministry. But
once there, he would spend long laborious hours trying to master the
intricacies and political complexities, the rights and wrongs of the
arguments that had preceded the Disruption, the follies perpetrated by
both factions in the General Assembly of the Church of Scotland—the
'Non-Intrusionists', who wanted no interference from the State in the
affairs of the Kirk, and the 'Moderates', who were against any action
that might lead to the disestablishment of the Kirk as the national
Church. However, Archie Charteris, the minister, was to discover all
too clearly the effects of that fateful Thursday in May 1843, when the
great Thomas Chalmers, the brilliant Church of Scotland minister,
orator and social worker, had led the dissenters from the General
Assembly meeting in St Andrews Church in Edinburgh, to set up 'The
Church of Scotland, Free and Protesting'.

At the time, however, all that Archie Charteris, the schoolboy, had
known about it was the charged air of excitement in Wamphray in the
months leading up to the Disruption. The village was bombarded with
leaflets from the Non-Intrusionists and the Moderates alike. Deputations from each side came to put their case from pulpit and public
platform, trying to persuade people to stay loyal to the old Kirk or to
support the 480 ministers who had pledged themselves to resign at the
next General Assembly. Young Archie did not have a very clear idea of
what the grown-ups were arguing about so heatedly; but there were
scuffles among the bigger boys in the schoolyard, and even boys of his
own age would shake a menacing fist in his face and demand, 'Are ye a
Non or a Mo?' They had no idea that a 'Non' was a Non-Intrusionist,
and that a 'Mo' was a Moderate—these were just handy labels, a good
excuse for squaring up in the playground. At home, Archie saw his
father, who was the session clerk of Wamphray Parish and a determined
Moderate, preparing and distributing for signatures a petition which
was presented to the Revd Charles Dickson (who had Non-Intrusionist
leanings), which entreated him 'to consider well the ecclesiastical
situation on constitutional lines, and not to be carried away by secession
fever or fear of reproach'.

Mr Dickson eventually heeded this advice, and 'stayed in' on the day
of the great walk-out from the General Assembly on 18 May 1843. The
following Sunday saw the great exodus of elders and congregations in

the parishes. Many of Mr Charles Dickson's congregation 'came out' and formed the Johnstone and Wamphray Free Church. Like most, they started without a place of worship, or any funds. Like many, they had no minister: ministers who 'came out' relinquished their churches, manses and stipends. But some ministers took entire congregations with them, while others who 'stayed in' were left with half-empty churches.

Archie Charteris will have noticed the empty pews in Wamphray Church, the boys and girls missing from Sunday school. He would see the tent being erected in the field behind Mr Little's house at Roughlake —that was where the Free congregation held their services for a while. Sadly, as happened in many cases, the Free-kirkers were ordered off by the landowner, and had to take refuge in an old barn which they fitted up as best they could in time to ordain their first minister, the Revd Peter Hope, in October 1844. The barn was exchanged for another tent before a sympathetic landowner granted them land, and a church and manse were built. The Free Church thrived, and Archie Charteris grew accustomed to there being three churches, three Sunday schools, three Bible classes, three annual treats, three Communion Days and Fast Days—all in that same, small country parish.

It would be 1900 before the Relief Church (which had by then united with earlier seceders as the United Presbyterian Church) joined forces with the Free Church to form the United Free Church. And Archie Charteris did not live to see the grand reunion of 1929, when the United Free Church returned to the fold and joined hands once more with the old Kirk. But he spent his life working to that end, campaigning tirelessly for the removal of patronage, which was finally achieved in 1874. The whole direction of his life and ministry was towards repairing the damage done in that catastrophic year of 1843 when he was a small boy of seven, and towards finding new sources of manpower —and womanpower—with which to revitalise his sorely stricken Church.

4

Mission Begun

Archie Charteris became a student at the University of Edinburgh when he was still a month short of his fourteenth birthday. He travelled by train from Wamphray in November 1849, and found lodgings in Edinburgh's Old Town, the heart of Church, University and Law, one of Europe's main cultural centres, the Athens of the North—but also in those days a seething insanitary huddle of overcrowded humanity. Despite the fresh winds blowing from the Pentland Hills and the sea on its doorstep, Edinburgh, like all the major cities of the time, was a hotbed of disease. Smallpox, typhus and cholera stalked its stinking wynds and regularly decimated the numbers of the hungry and the destitute who were crowded into the closely-packed 'lands' or tenements. As fast as they died, others came to take their place, flocking in from the country in search of work, easy prey to the germs and bacteria that thrived in houses without sanitation of any kind, in choked drains, in untreated sewage, in streets and closes deep in filth.

Edinburgh's medical school was renowned the world over, and its doctors were on the brink of discoveries that would one day alleviate and prevent the suffering and pestilence, not only in Edinburgh but throughout the world. Joseph Lister, a brilliant young English surgeon, was working as assistant to the great Scottish surgeon James Syme, professor of Clinical Surgery (who was, incidentally, the man who invented the method of waterproofing that was later to be patented by Mackintosh): by 1860, Lister would have introduced antiseptics, which vastly increased the safety of surgical operations and revolutionised attitudes to health and hygiene in hospitals, homes and public places. James Young Simpson from Bathgate—the obstetrician, founder of gynaecology, and hospital reformer—was professor of Midwifery and had just begun to use ether as an anaesthetic in childbirth. He had also discovered the properties of chloroform by experimenting on himself, but he was still having to champion its cause against medical and

28

religious opposition and chloroform was not to be accepted in general until after it had been used by Queen Victoria at the birth of her youngest son, Prince Leopold, in 1853.

So in hospital was not the safest place to be when Archie Charteris was a student in Edinburgh. General hospitals, run on charity, were incapable of coping with epidemics of plague, and could offer neither hope nor facilities for the growing army of sufferers from the scourge that was to haunt the Western world for the next century—tuberculosis. There was little treatment or alleviation for TB, and there would be no cure until the development of antibiotics in the 1940s. Victorians, rich and poor, accepted TB (or 'consumption' as it was called) as a fact of life; a death sentence from which there could be no reprieve. They watched their large families being regularly and cruelly cut down, and the children's names were transferred year after year from the big family Bibles to the long lists on family headstones in cemeteries and churchyards. People learned to recognise the tell-tale signs of the disease on cheek and brow, and even in the nature and character of the child or young adult; they described the marked one euphemistically as 'a delicate child' or 'fast ripening for glory' or 'a child on whom God's seal is set'. Such language may sound extravagant, even faintly ridiculous, to our ears; but such images, along with their songs of hope and their hymns promising 'a happy land far, far away', are a moving testimony to the courage of those amazing Victorians, who lost so much without faltering in their faith.

Young Archie Charteris, fresh from the clean sweet mountain air of Upper Annandale, contracted nothing lethal during eight years of studying in Edinburgh. But he never enjoyed really good health from then on. Most of his adult life was beset by illness of one kind or another, ranging from blinding headaches (probably what we would now call migraine) to sciatica, neuritis and other unidentified aches and pains. Illness and overwork caused him to have repeated breakdowns at university, and forced him to take a year off his studies and stay at home in Wamphray, where he helped his father in the schoolroom and spent as much time as possible out of doors. He was by far the youngest of his university year (one of his classmates was eight years his senior), and he suffered severely from sheer examination fright as well as ill-health. He sat one exam with a dozen leeches attached to his head, yet managed to come out third in the prize-list. He was twice among the prize-winners in his first session, and four times in the last year of his Master of Arts course, before going on to the four year course in Divinity. A certificate presented to him by Professor James Pillans (Humanities) declared:

He stands in the foremost rank of all the pupils I have ever had for every quality to be desired of a student: uniform propriety of conduct, unremitting attention in the class-room, industry at home, and ability far above common.

In fact, Charteris was too ill to complete the two extra subjects required to turn his BA degree into an MA. It was not until 1854, during his first year in Divinity Hall, that he was able to take the full degree.

Throughout his eight years in Edinburgh, Charteris was helping to pay his own way by tutoring schoolboys. There were no grants or bursaries in those days. Every penny had to be earned, or sent from home:

[Eight pounds] will do me just now for class tickets and matriculation, and I have plenty of change for some time. The library I do not need as yet until salary time, so you need not send any more, but just write me. . . .

Is not all this providential? about eight hours' tutoring if I wished it, whilst scores of poor fellows have nothing. Of course four or five hours will be my utmost. Though I am more favourably situated than most students, there is a feeling of outsideness in tutoring which I cannot get over. I dinna like it.[1]

He also taught Sunday school in the Tron Church and at St Stephen's in the New Town, where he saw women taking part in congregational activities to an extent that was unusual for the times. He was a regular church attender, took his first Communion at Wamphray when he was 18 years old, and like other Divinity students did a lot of 'sermon-tasting' in Edinburgh, going round the churches to sample the preaching skills of some of the greatest preachers of their, or any other, day. He found the celebrated Norman Candlish, successor to Chalmers in the leadership of the Free Church, 'abrupt and ill at his ease in a pulpit'. Dr John Caird, however, whom Charteris would one day succeed as minister of Park Church in Glasgow, was 'first rate . . . he really deserves his reputation, great as it is'.[2]

He attended political meetings and public lectures. He listened to a political oration by the author and statesman, Lord Macaulay, who was MP for Edinburgh at the time. He heard Dickens reading his *Christmas Carol*. He heard Thackeray giving readings from his own novels. And all the time his eyes were being opened and his heart was being moved by the plight of the people around him in the teeming Old Town: the abject poverty, the dirt and disease, the drunkenness, the crime, the ragged and starving children; the hopelessness, the Godlessness of it all, the empty dilapidated churches—and the apparent inability of his own Church, the Established Church of Scotland, depleted in numbers and resources by the Disruption, to cope with the needs of the people.

He joined the University Missionary Association and became its president in his final year. It met on Saturday mornings, and was run by the leading theological students as part of the practical side of their training. It too had been greatly weakened by the Disruption, but was now gathering strength and influence again. It was contributing towards the maintenance of a missionary abroad, and Archie Charteris, still in his teens, became the leader of a campaign to revive Edinburgh churches where the few members left after the Disruption could not afford to pay a minister nor maintain the building. They started with the historic old Chapel of Buccleuch in the parish of St Cuthbert's. It had fallen into dilapidation, and there was nowhere for the poor folk of the area to worship. The students undertook to provide the larger part of the minister's stipend, and the kirk session of St Cuthbert's allowed them to appoint the Revd Alexander McLaren. They supported him by attending his services in large numbers and organised systematic visiting round the district, encouraging folk to come to church and making them feel welcome when they came. Soon large congregations were filling the old church, and the success of the experiment raised hopes that the tide had turned in the fortunes of the Church of Scotland in Edinburgh.

For Charteris, who was made president of the Missionary Association in recognition of his part in the project, this was a taste of the work that was to be his life. It was the first intimation of his qualities of leadership, of his skill at organisation, of his knack of seeing what had to be done—and then going out and doing it. Already he was groping his way towards what he called 'applied Christianity' and sometimes 'Clinical Divinity', seeking an analogy in scientific terms for his growing conviction that being a minister was not just a matter of preaching a good sermon, and that being a Christian was not just a matter of sitting and listening to those sermons. Charteris wanted everyone to be up and doing, every day. There was work to be done. Faith must be turned into action, theology must be put into practice, if the masses outside the Church, both at home and abroad, were to be brought into the fold and their lives uplifted, socially as well as spiritually.

Such were the ideas tumbling around in his head during those student years—ideas mixed with the doubts and uncertainties of a young man who had gone straight from childhood to manhood without any teenage or between-age of fun and freedom. From a 13 year old climbing trees in Wamphray Glen he had become overnight 'Mr Charteris', living alone in a strange city with the responsibility for his own upkeep; serious matters were to be debated and worried over and confided to his diary:

> Am I fit to be a minister? Mr John G says: Every man should lead a minister's life, and the man who is not fit for a minister is not fit for anything good. True enough, but this merely proves that no man should be other than a Christian: it by no means proves that non-Christians should be ministers. . . .
> Have felt uneasy and not piously inclined today. Although feeling my dependence on God, have been unable to compose my mind sufficiently. Lord, I am weak; help me![3]

That entry had been written in Wamphray on the eve of a new session at the university. Next day he was on the train to Edinburgh again, carrying with him something which alleviated the austerity of his college life and possibly saved him from even worse ill-health: his 'box from home', a weekly or fortnightly supply of nourishing country fare provided by his mother to ensure that he was well fed, and to save him money. Eggs, potatoes, cabbages, leeks, fruits in season and home-baking—these were all packed in, along with his weekly wash, and despatched to him by train:

> My box came today. Everything in tip-top order. Never saw less breakage, even the oatcakes all unfractured. Eggs whole except one, which I broke myself in unpacking; but I have it in a cup for a fry. . . .
> My last bit of cake will be swallowed before this letter is posted. I am very sparing of them: 'better long something than soon naething'.

Charteris appreciated the good country fare so much that it must have underlined the inadequate diet of the poor folk he met on his visits round the slums neighbouring Buccleuch Church; and one of the first concerted efforts that the Woman's Guild was to make was the weekly despatch from country parishes of eggs, cabbages and flowers to be sold for a few pence to people who could not afford the high costs in city shops.

Charteris was 22 years old when he finished his Divinity course; and on 24 February 1858, he was duly licensed as the Revd A H Charteris. He would dearly have loved to be a foreign missionary, but his health was not good enough; he was offered a chaplaincy in India, but had to decline. At home there were no assistant ministers in those days, unless they were preparing to take over from a retiring incumbent, so there were few opportunities for an apprenticeship to break a new pro-bationer into parish work under the guidance of an experienced minister. Charteris had to take what chance he could of preaching, and hope that he would be noticed by some laird on the look-out for a new man for one of his parish pulpits. The nightmare was to become a 'stickit minister'—a probationer who remained a probationer for the rest of his life. But after only his third appearance in a pulpit—standing in for a friend in Ayr—Charteris was invited to the Caledonian Hotel in Edinburgh to meet his first patron: Mr Alexander Haldane Oswald MP, of Auchencruive. Mr Oswald offered him a church on his estate.

According to his own description, Mr Oswald 'drew ample revenues from widespread territories' in Ayrshire and Galloway, and was now needing an assistant to the Revd Dr Stair M'Quhae at St Quivox (now in Prestwick, but at that time a country and mining parish near Ayr). Dr M'Quhae was the son of a minister who had been described by Robert Burns as 'that cursed rascal called M'Quhae'; father and son had been in charge at St Quivox for a hundred years.

The call from the St Quivox congregation was signed by four elders and 56 members on 29 April 1858. The new minister's old professor of Church History, Dr James Robertson, joined with the Presbytery in the solemn ritual of 'laying on of hands' at his ordination. His mother was also present. The Revd A H Charteris then moved into a corner of Dr M'Quhae's well-appointed manse to begin his first ministry. His stipend was £120, half of which was paid by the heritors (Mr Oswald and two others) and half by Dr M'Quhae.

He was 22 years old, and very frightened.

Notes to Chapter 4

1 Arthur Gordon, *The Life of Archibald Hamilton Charteris* (Hodder & Stoughton, 1913), pp 19–20
2 ibid, p 22
3 ibid, p 23

5

Lady Grisell

What alarmed Archie Charteris most about his new parish was that so many of its inhabitants were miners; for miners in those days were thought of as alien beings, strange dark creatures who scrabbled in the bowels of the earth—coarse, illiterate, aggressive louts who gambled and swore and shunned all but their own kind:

> I was in literal terror of the colliers. I had never seen one any more than I had seen a Roman Catholic in my life, and I believed that the colliers would stone or taunt me as I went through Whitletts, their village on the high road from Ayr, with 1200 inhabitants. The first time I walked up the long street I kept the middle of the highway (as we used to do in the earlier days when we were afraid of ghosts), so that if an assailant came from either side I would get a start and run before he could get at me. And I nervously watched the doorways in which curious women stood, each looking quite innocent with a needle and a bit of dirty crochet in her hand. I did not expect to find so many friends in those one-roomed houses as in a short time I found to my great joy.[1]

He only stayed for 13 months in St Quivox; but by the end of that time he had 60 married miners attending his class for first communicants:

> . . . anxiously trying to take in my Christian teaching, living sober lives, and never absent from church on a Sunday. They were pathetically anxious to learn, and although one of the elders said I might as well preach in Greek for anything the colliers would understand, they soon came to take in bits of my sermons. In the class I could soon tell how much or how little they understood. True, loyal, loving souls they were; living a hard and joyless life in the pits.[2]

He was saddened by the great gulf that existed between the colliers and the farm people:

> There was no alliance between the two divisions. There was not even acquaintance. The colliers were little cared for, their cottages were far

below the Ayrshire average in accommodation and comfort, and the men themselves were personally unknown outside of their villages. Every farmer's boy thought himself far above the 'coalers'.[3]

But at least the 'farm people' were extraordinarily kind to the new minister. They knew the heavy expense of playing host to visiting preachers, particularly during the three days of special services in the Communion season, and they saw to it that he had a good supply of turkeys, geese and chickens for the manse table. On the way to Church on Sundays they would look into his coal-house ('after taking their statutory drink at the manse pump'), and if it was less than full they would bring coals the next day.

The pews were well filled during his year at St Quivox. He began to gain a reputation as a rising young preacher, and the children loved him. As one old man was to put it in later years: 'He drew a terrible heap of young ones after him'. But running what were in effect two parishes—the farming one and the mining community, each with its own separate Sunday schools and adult classes—began to tell on his health. So when a small country parish was offered to him, he was advised on health grounds to accept—and he did.

But Charteris had another reason for accepting: for he was being offered the parish of New Abbey in the Presbytery of Dumfries and Kirkcudbright, and his great-uncle, the Revd James Hamilton (the one who had fired the shots at Burns' funeral), had ministered there for 45 years. It had been his dying wish that young Archie should succeed him at New Abbey.

New Abbey was a truly rural parish on the Solway Firth; the sea was only half a mile from the manse at high tide, and eight miles away when the tide was out. Charteris found it 'the loveliest of parishes' and went everywhere on horseback, his pony following him like a dog whenever he dismounted. The hills and the lochs and the daily exercise in the fresh air soon brought back something like the robust health of his childhood. Later, he was to write of the five years he spent at New Abbey: 'In no other five years of my life have I existed without a doctor's prescription'.

One of the first things he did was to organise a campaign to save Sweetheart Abbey, the ruined Cistercian abbey adjoining New Abbey Church. The thirteenth century abbey had been built by Devorgilla, Lady of Galloway, who had buried there the 'sweet heart' of her husband, John Balliol, father of that brief King of Scotland, John 'Toom Tabard' Balliol. It was already a ruin, albeit a beautiful, romantic ruin, and Charteris was anxious to ensure that something be done quickly to prevent the complete collapse of the walls. Showing the initiative for action that was already becoming a marked characteristic, he summoned a meeting in the manse, invited the Press to attend, and raised £400 on the spot. In no time at all he had a squad of masons at work, stopping up gaps in the stonework with cement and restoring some of the damaged mullions in the empty windows.

Sweetheart Abbey, which has been in the care of the Secretary of State for Scotland since 1928, is now one of the gems in the estate administered by the Historic Buildings and Monuments Directorate on behalf of the nation. Thousands visit it every year, marvelling at the beauty and grandeur of its 700 year old ruins. It is heart-warming to reflect that Sweetheart Abbey might never have survived in its present state had it not been for the resourcefulness of a young minister called Charteris, who was already 'mighty busy with other things'.

Charteris developed greatly as a preacher while he was at New Abbey. Churches in nearby Dumfries were always crowded when he went to preach there; sometimes people had to be turned away at the doors. He was also much in demand as a public speaker, and wrote literary reviews for the Edinburgh *Evening Courant*. But above all, this was the time when he began to identify more clearly his real mission in life. He was beginning to realise that it was up to the younger ministers of the Church of Scotland to rouse the old Kirk from its torpor and reach out to the masses who were outside her influence and care. In a letter to a fellow-minister he wrote: 'Something must be done—aye, everything must be done—if the old ship is to hold together for ten years longer'.

He threw himself eagerly into the Endowment Scheme for new parishes, which had been started a few years after the Disruption by his old professor and hero, Dr James Robertson. The purpose of the Endowment Scheme was to raise money, not only to provide a church and maintain a minister in each new parish, but, in Charteris' words, 'to fill the whole church in the pulpit and the pew with the spirit of a new ideal'. He became Dr Robertson's lieutenant in the campaign, organising and addressing meetings all over the country, raising funds in his own parish and going on deputations to other presbyteries. He made his first speech at the General Assembly of 1860 with 'a high-toned and well-reasoned appeal' in support of Endowment; and when 'Endowment Robertson' died that same year, the fund-raising went on with increased fervour, so that by 1870 Robertson's dream of 150 new Church of Scotland parishes had been established by endowment. By 1907 another 300 had been added, giving the old Kirk 247 942 new communicants and an added population of well over two million in the new parishes.

During those early years of campaigning for the Endowment Scheme, Charteris went on a deputation to Aberdeen in the company of Major, the Honourable Robert Baillie of Mellerstain and Dryburgh, brother of the 10th Earl of Haddington, elder of Bowden Presbyterian Church near St Boswells, and founder of the Border Elders' Union. Major Baillie was a man of such saintly character and handsome looks that only the Victorians could have found the words to describe him. Charteris' biographer, the Revd Arthur Gordon, called Major Baillie 'the unconscious Sir Galahad of the beautiful face and knightly bearing'[4]. Charteris himself wrote, 'The Major led an ideal life as clear as the crystal tones of his voice and the liquid softness of his eye'. Major Baillie was to become a great friend and supporter of the schoolmaster's son from Wamphray, championing his causes, working for his schemes, backing him in the face of any opposition.

Perhaps the greatest favour he bestowed on Charteris in the New Abbey days was to introduce him to his youngest sister, Lady Grisell Baillie, who would later become the First Lady, one might say, of the Woman's Guild. Her beauty and goodness were renowned in the Border country and, if possible, eclipsed even her brother's. Lady Grisell was the youngest of the remarkable Baillie family of 11 children. Their father, one-time Member of Parliament for Berwickshire, was a descendant of the Scottish church martyr, Baillie of Jerviswood. Their maternal grandmother was a Macleod of Macleod, and they had inherited their striking good looks from both sides of the family. The eldest of the six sons, George, became the 10th Earl of Haddington; the eldest of the five beautiful daughters, Eliza, became Marchioness of Breadalbane. One married the Earl of Ashburnham, another married the Earl of Aberdeen, another became Lady Polwarth. Only Grisell of the five sisters never married.

Grisell was so beautiful as a six year old that her mother could not take her out in the streets of Edinburgh without being 'incommoded by the notice the child attracted'. One of her sisters described her thus:

> Radiant beauty are the only words which express the effect produced by the roses and lilies of her complexion, the brilliancy of the sparkling eyes, the calmness of the fair open brow, the rounded cheeks, the sunny hair, the Hebe-like joyousness of the expression, the slight, graceful figure, with the air of distinction which possessed her to the last.[5]

When she was 22 years old her portrait was drawn by the artist J R Swinton, and now hangs in the Scottish National Portrait Gallery in Edinburgh. The Gallery also has in its possession a photograph of her, one of the earliest photographs ever taken, which was published in the celebrated Hill and Adamson collection entitled *An Early Victorian Album.*

Lady Grisell was in her late thirties when Charteris first met her. She was unmarried, although there had been many offers, and she lived at home with her widowed mother and two unmarried brothers: Thomas, 'The Admiral', and Robert, 'The Major'. They had relinquished the family seat of Mellerstain to the eldest son, and stayed in various houses before renting Dryburgh Abbey House as their home. It was when Grisell was 25 that 'the strong hand of the Almighty was stretched forth for [her] salvation', although 'it was not, however, till near the end of 1848 that [she] confessed Christ'. The Major made the same decision a year later and, having left the army 'for his widowed mother's sake and for Christ's sake', he made a pact with his sister to 'walk together' in a life devoted to prayer, praise, Bible-reading and Christian service.

It was a remarkable partnership, which Lady Grisell described in ecstatically glowing terms in a tribute she penned to her brother after his death (*Recollections of a Happy Life: Begun on Earth, Made Perfect in the Skies*):

> There was never a cloud between us. In him were all the fruits of the Spirit—love, joy, peace, gentleness, goodness, meekness, poverty of spirit, humility in its fairest form, the broken and contrite spirit in which God delights. . . .
>
> He and I breakfasted together at 8.30 all the year round. Mirthful happy joyous breakfast-time! . . . Every day, morning and night, from 3rd June, 1854, the day after he was ordained an elder, he conducted family worship. . . .
>
> I read to him daily, immediately after our morning prayer, a Psalm, a portion from the Prophets, Gospels and Epistles. Also I repeated to him the texts from *Daily Food*. He then prayed over each portion. Such teaching! Such lessons! . . .
>
> Our talk as we walked by the way was of God's word. He always prayed with me when we came in from our walk, before dinner, and always immediately after dinner, and the last thing at night. He never left me to go out walking alone without praying for me before he went.[6]

But their life was not all praise and prayer and Bible-reading. It was packed with action and activity. They were busy all day on errands of mercy among the sick and the poor folk of the parish. The Major was not one of your twice-a-year-visiting elders. He visited every day, and Lady Grisell went with him, carrying baskets of food, bunches of flowers, medicine, cast-off clothes and edifying books. For almost 50 years, brother and sister taught in the Sunday school at Bowden Church, and Lady Grisell held informal meetings for young women on Sunday afternoons. She started a branch of the YWCA in the district, organised a united foreign missionary agency in which the Church of Scotland, Free Church and United Presbyterian could all work together, and promoted an annual sale in St Boswells to raise funds for overseas work. She started a Mother's Meeting in Newtown St Boswells, and provided a water supply for the village at her own expense. She also paid for the building of a bridge over the River Tweed when there was no way to cross except by ferry.

Was it Lady Grisell's extraordinary example that inspired Charteris to conceive of a whole army of churchwomen at work? Certainly, he must have been enormously impressed by what one woman could do to spread the Word and put her faith into action in the parish—latterly on her own, for when the Major died she took on the entire visitation of the parishioners in his elder's district, on top of all her other work. No wonder Charteris selected her as the first candidate for his new Order of Deaconesses.

But there were to be many changes in his own life before that came about. As his reputation at New Abbey grew, he was pressed to accept more important charges in various parts of the country. There were at least a dozen offers, but he turned them all down, preferring to stay in his lovely country parish and continue his work for the endowment of new churches. Then, in 1863, Dr John Caird, 'the prince of Scottish preachers', was appointed to the Chair of Divinity at the University of Glasgow, leaving a vacancy in Park Church in the West End of Glasgow. A deputation from Park Church appeared in New Abbey Church one Sunday, and a few days later Lord Provost Clouston arrived in person to offer Mr Charteris Park Church. This time he accepted, because of what he called 'my loyalty to Dr Robertson and the Endowment Scheme'.

Park was one of the two wealthiest churches in Glasgow. The other was Sandyford, and Charteris thought it wrong that both were still only chapels, unendowed, self-supporting, and with no allegiance to a parish. He agreed to go to Park on condition that the congregation should 'endow church and district for territorial work within a year'. His terms were accepted, and within three months the congregation had raised the sum required for endowment: Park Church became The Park Parish, and in that congregation of what Charteris called 'the elite of the public men of Glasgow, lawyers, merchants, bankers, retired ministers, active professors', a certain number of free pews was set aside for the use of the poor.

But before the Revd A H Charteris could take up his new appointment, he had another appointment to keep—his wedding to the woman who was to become the first president of the Woman's Guild.

Notes to Chapter 5

1 Arthur Gordon, *The Life of Archibald Hamilton Charteris* (Hodder & Stoughton, 1913), p 49
2 ibid, p 52
3 ibid, p 51
4 ibid, p 356
5 D P Thomson, *Women of the Scottish Church* (Perth, 1975), p 291
6 ibid, p 293

6

Married Life and Work

Catherine Morice Anderson was 23 years old when she first met the young minister from New Abbey. Charteris was then 25, and was visiting Aberdeen to research a biography of his old friend and mentor, 'Endowment' Robertson. Professor Robertson had been a native of Aberdeen, and Charteris had travelled north to interview some of the professor's old friends and colleagues. One of these was the Lord Provost of Aberdeen, Sir Alexander Anderson, the most eminent Aberdonian of his day and the man most responsible for the tremendous development of the city in the middle of the nineteenth century.

It was Anderson's enterprise and business flair that brought Aberdeen the Great North Railway and the North Eastern line connecting Aberdeen with Montrose and Brechin; the North of Scotland Bank and the Northern Assurance Company; the Aberdeen Market; the water supply from the upper reaches of the River Dee; a fine new Grammar School, and the city's handsome Municipal and County Buildings. Aberdeen's splendid 'West-end' housing development was started through his purchase of Rubislaw estate, and he masterminded the development of Torry as a suburb for people working in the rapidly growing fishing industry. Aberdeen's handsome rose-lined dual carriageway, Anderson Drive, is named after Lord Provost Sir Alexander Anderson.

The Lord Provost had two daughters, Catherine and Helen. Catherine, the elder of the two, captivated the young minister from the moment they met. She was no outstanding beauty; she had neither the saintly looks of a Lady Grisell, nor the shy blushes of the country maiden, nor the genteel politeness of the Edinburgh drawing-room. She was a down-to-earth, no-nonsense Aberdeen lassie, highly intelligent, very well educated, with a keen sense of humour, a ready wit and a warm heart. Her mother's health was poor, and Catherine was well used to playing hostess to the important businessmen, civic dignitaries and leaders of church and university who were the Lord Provost's guests. Small and neat, with high cheek-bones and a broad, generous mouth, she had a friendly, open, almost man-to-man style in conversation that was unusual in an age when women's opinions were seldom invited or offered. She could hold her own in any company, in a way that was unorthodox without being unladylike. She could match witticism with witticism, even when the male repartee was in scholarly Latin.

Altogether she was like a breath of fresh, clean, invigorating North Sea air; and a year after they first met, Archie Charteris proposed to her one July morning on a climb to the top of the hill of Morven. They were married on 24 November 1863, in the Lord Provost's parlour. They had thought of having the ceremony in the bride's church, the beautiful old West Parish of St Nicholas, but church weddings were still a new-fangled idea in Presbyterian Scotland, and the young couple settled for an old-fashioned marriage ceremony at home. After a three day honeymoon in Kincardineshire they went straight to Glasgow, where the Park kirk session had rented a furnished house for them in Ashton Terrace, off what is now busy Byres Road. At that time it was practically out in the country—in fact, Lord Provost Anderson addressed his first letter to the newly-weds 'Opposite the Haystack, Glasgow', and it arrived safely! Later they moved to a house in Crown Circus, Dowanhill; it was nearly two miles from the church, and a further two miles from Park to the slums of Port Dundas, where Charteris had permission to run a Mission in the Barony parish of Dr Norman Macleod. This was the opportunity he wanted 'to introduce his own wealthy church members to work among the poorer classes', as his biographer put it.

In Port Dundas, Charteris organised Sunday schools and Bible classes, adult classes and mothers' meetings, and teams of workers from his West End kirk to run things. Mrs Charteris and a band of Park women, most of whom had never ventured down-town in their lives, beat a regular path to Port Dundas, visiting homes and running meetings in both parishes, as well as running Dorcas meetings where they sewed and repaired clothing for their Mission friends. One of his young parishioners, Miss Jane Houldsworth, told later how much she and her sisters owed to Mr Charteris for giving them the opportunity to do this work:

> . . . by his persuasion our mother allowed us to visit among the poor, in the crowded East-end district of Port Dundas. My sisters and myself had wished it, but had not been allowed till Mr Charteris came. In those days

the slums of the East end were not considered suitable for young girls to walk and visit in. But we got a start in the work through the quiet, almost silent, influence of our new young minister. Our lives from that date began to be much more useful, and *much* more happy.[1]

Mr Charteris persuaded West End families to 'adopt' East End ones; the Houldsworth family took charge of an orphan brother and sister, fed them and clothed them, and took them on outings. As for the minister himself, every day was crammed with congregational and parish visiting, meetings of the kirk session, appearances at mothers' meetings, teaching in Bible classes, presiding at a Literary Society which he founded at Park, and visiting the Working Men's Institute at Port Dundas. On Sundays he preached morning and afternoon at Park, then he and his wife were off to Port Dundas for Sunday schools and Sunday worship there.

And not unexpectedly, the inevitable happened: within 18 months his health broke down, and Charteris was off work for nine months. He and his wife went to Sicily and the Italian mainland, where Mrs Charteris was stricken with fever (probably typhoid) and had to be rushed home. Charteris went on by himself to Switzerland, where 'my terrible, disabling headaches became at least intermittent. When I returned to Scotland, the heather and the sweet air of Deeside drove them away'. He returned to Glasgow and threw himself once more into an operation that was unlike anything seen before in a prosperous West End parish. He had an assistant minister, a team of elders and an enthusiastic band of women working in the West End, and another assistant minister, another team of elders, some specially ordained deacons and another band of women working at Port Dundas. As one of the assistants, the Revd W Jardine Dobie, put it: 'Under his guiding hand the organisation was of the most complete and perfect kind'.

Yet Mr Dobie often found Charteris prostrated with severe sciatica, 'lying helpless on his bed, only able to move with the assistance of a cord carried over a pulley . . .'. As the work increased, the bouts of illness recurred more frequently. Holidays in a warm climate was the doctor's prescription; and it was through these that Charteris' lifetime of ill-health became a blessing in disguise, because the enforced sojourns on the Continent gave him an opportunity to see the way that women worked in other European Churches. He was particularly interested in the Deaconess Order, which he found operating in almost every Protestant country in western Europe except Scotland. The more he saw of these dedicated full-time women workers, the more he became convinced that this was what the Church of Scotland needed —but not Deaconesses alone. He was seeing in the work going on at

Park and at Port Dundas in Glasgow the tremendous power that was
unleashed when women with homes and families and domestic responsibilities, as well as women with no real job of work to do, were given
the opportunity for action and service in the community. They were
often powerful evangelists. They were more readily accepted on
Mission visits than men. They were not just talkers, but could nurse the
baby, or cook a meal, or apply a poultice. Charteris dreamed of
harnessing the vast untapped potential of women who were sitting
demurely and passively in a thousand churches all over Scotland: a great
pyramid of part-time church workers, rising up to a summit of
highly-trained, full-time Deaconesses.

He knew there were years of groundwork ahead; years of encouraging the kind of work going on at Park and a few other outstanding
parishes; years of preaching, of education, of changing men's attitudes
and women's ingrained sense of inferiority.

All his dreams almost came to nothing, however, and the Woman's
Guild might never have come into being, because of something that
happened during a holiday in Germany in the summer of 1868. As
Charteris was embarking at Hamburg, he fell through some rotten
wood on the pier and plunged into the water. A strong current swept
him away, and he very nearly drowned before he was rescued in the
nick of time. He suffered three broken ribs, and shock; but only two
days later he was preaching in Glasgow. His brave show fooled no one,
not even himself. It was obvious that the strain of running two parishes
was simply too much for him; and when he was offered the Chair
of Biblical Criticism at the University of Edinburgh, he accepted,
becoming a professor at the age of 33.

He preached his last sermon at Park on 2 October 1868; but if Mrs
Charteris looked forward to her husband enjoying a quiet academic life
free of the hassle and responsibilities of parish work, she was not long in
learning her mistake. After a year of settling in at the university and
living quietly at 44 Inverleith Row in the New Town, Professor
Charteris was turning his attention to the slums of the Old Town, in
particular those dark tenements crammed between the Lawnmarket
and the Mound at the top of the Royal Mile. They were populated by
the poorest, sorriest souls in the city; and in the centre of all the
degradation and neglect stood the proud, lofty spire of Tolbooth St
John's Church. It had been built only 25 years earlier as Victoria Hall, to
accommodate the General Assembly of the Church of Scotland; but for
most of the year it stood there empty and aloof, an ironic comment on
the Church's failure to grapple with the pressing social and spiritual
needs of the unchurched masses living round its doors. It was neither

parish church nor chapel; it had no ministers, no endowment; it had only 25 members, on whom newly-licensed young ministers without a church practised their preaching on Sundays.

Professor Charteris resolved to raise the Tolbooth as Buccleuch Church had been rescued in his student days. He appealed once again to the University Missionary Association and quickly formed a team of students—most of them his Biblical Criticism class, but with medical, law and arts students as well. Around them rallied a great band of church workers, with Mrs Charteris leading the women. As Professor Charteris preached in the Tolbooth, Sunday after Sunday, crowds flocked to listen—and many stayed to help. A young licentiate, the Revd Peter Thomson, later minister of Dunning in Perthshire, was appointed missionary; but the presbytery gave Professor Charteris authority to administer the sacraments at the Tolbooth, and from 1870 to 1872 he was in effect the unpaid minister of the district, as well as directing the whole operation of the mission.

He trained his students and other team-workers in the art of visiting the poor people of the Lawnmarket: how to approach with tact and courtesy; to be sympathetic without being patronising; not to preach, or use religious jargon; discreetly to discover secret needs and worries; never to stay too long in any one house. It was just the sort of advice that is handed out to elders today with all the benefits of modern psychological study and social work experience. Indeed, the whole Charteris exercise could give pointers to any modern social work department in the thoroughness of its organisation, the careful keeping of records, the regularity of visiting, and the personal attention given to every member of every family. Each visitor had a district book and kept a regular diary of fortnightly visits, the particular needs of each family, the names of the children, the state of their health. It was Mrs Charteris' job to keep two large volumes, with two or three pages devoted to each family and regularly updated from the visitors' reports. These were, in reality, case histories, long before the term 'case history' was coined. A fortnightly meeting of all the workers discussed specific cases and decided on the help to be given: clothes, money, advice, spiritual guidance.

Charteris was at pains to co-operate with other churches in the area, such as Free St John's and Free Tolbooth, to avoid duplicating the Mission work. He was well aware that people sometimes tried to play one church off against another: he told of a case where a man died, and three different churches each provided a coffin. In another instance a widow 'found seven different streams of charity flowing' to her and her four children, with the result that in her affluence she took to drink and became a confirmed drunkard.

Drink, vice and crime were rife in the dark wynds and vennels of the
Lawnmarket, and sometimes the police had to be called in; but the
Tolbooth workers managed to hold stairhead services and back-court
meetings unmolested, and on Sunday evenings in the church there was
a service which was open only to those wearing 'moleskins and
working-clothes, or with shawls over their heads instead of bonnets'.
In a few years the number of communicants at Tolbooth had risen from
25 to 400—of whom 200 were from the Mission district. Upwards of
100 attended the weekly congregational prayer meeting. There was a
thriving Sunday school, a children's church (that was one of Charteris'
favourite ideas), a Young Men's Fellowship, Mrs Charteris' Bible class,
Mrs Charteris' mothers' meeting, a Saturday night musical entertainment, a clothing society, a work society, a savings bank with 386
depositors, and a congregational library.

Perhaps the most enterprising project in all this pioneering experiment in voluntary social welfare was a Social Club. It was a completely
new idea for its time, and was aimed at letting families enjoy each
other's company and some refreshment in congenial surroundings
untainted by strong drink. The premises were a first floor flat in the
Lawnmarket, which had been a particularly disreputable shebeen. For
the Social Club, it was renamed The Holly Tree; its rooms were
tastefully decorated and furnished by friends and well-wishers; its
dining-room supplied good wholesome food and excellent tea and
coffee. Professor Charteris supervised all the arrangements, and often
took his lunch there. Mrs Charteris was in charge of the accounts.
There was a manager and his wife, and a committee of management.
Admission was a halfpenny, and there was a reading room, a games
room, a wash room, and a writing room which had once served Robert
Burns as a bedroom. There was even a stock of wallpaper, which
customers could buy at reduced prices to brighten up their dingy
tenement homes; but this enterprise had to be abandoned, because as
soon as the houses were improved, the landlords put up the rents.
About 15 years later, when the Woman's Guild came up against the
same problem, a more radical plan was adopted: the slum houses
themselves were bought and refurbished, and then let to the needy at
reasonable rents.

By 1873 the Tolbooth Church had been endowed and raised to parish
status, and had ordained and installed its own minister, the Revd
George Wilson. The University Missionary Association turned its
attention to other needy areas, but the work of Mission continued
unabated in the Lawnmarket, and generations of divinity students went
to parishes throughout Scotland inspired and trained by the Tolbooth

experiment to do similar work in other parts of the country—and in other countries as well, as far afield as Australia.

Encouraged by the Tolbooth success and the tremendous energy it had unleashed in one Edinburgh parish (and inspired, too, by the wave of religious fervour whipped up by the visit to Scotland in 1873 of the American evangelists, Moody and Sankey), Charteris began his campaign to put the whole Church to work. As early as 1869, along with his friend Major Baillie, he had persuaded the General Assembly to form a Committee on Christian Life and Work, which was to become the powerhouse for all his schemes to harness the energies and enthusiasms of every man and woman in the Church of Scotland into an efficient, highly organised Christian force. Through his Christian Life and Work Committee, Charteris gave the Church such innovations as Quinquennial Visitations, Disjunction Certificates, the *Life and Work* magazine, the *Church of Scotland Year-Book*, visiting deputies, and Missions to the Highlands, to farm servants, and to Scots fisherfolk.

In 1880 the General Assembly agreed to the foundation of a Young Men's Guild; Charteris' ultimate effort to rally the male members of the Church for Christian fellowship, evangelism, discussion and debate (shades of the Wamphray Gabbing School!), and to befriend young men from the country who were coming to the cities to find work. With Charteris as president it went from strength to strength, providing Sunday school teachers, elders, community leaders, missionaries, and recruits for the ministry. It raised funds for foreign missions, and in 1889 sent one of its members, the Revd John Alexander Graham, to great things in India as the first Guild-sponsored foreign missionary.

By 1911 the Young Men's Guild had 30 867 members in 658 parishes. It never reached the proportions in size or service or influence that the Woman's Guild was to achieve, perhaps because it was only for *young* men, who were able to move on to eldership and other opportunities for service. The Young Men's Guild was a means to an end, whereas the Woman's Guild would be an end in itself—the only opportunity, apart from foreign missions, for women to participate in the affairs of the Church. The Young Men's Guild petered out between the two World Wars; but by then it had injected new vitality and purpose into the Church, and its initial success was to be a tremendous fillip for Charteris when he came at last to put before the General Assembly his Grand Plan for the women of the Church.

Note to Chapter 6

1 Arthur Gordon, *The Life of Archibald Hamilton Charteris* (Hodder & Stoughton, 1913), p 105

7

The Assembly Says 'Yes'

When Professor Charteris stood up to address the 1885 General Assembly of the Church of Scotland, there was an expectant stir among the Fathers and Brethren. They had all read his latest report for the Christian Life and Work Committee, and they were ready for fireworks—and a bit of fun. It was always the same. The changes his committee were making, or wanted to make, in the life of the Church were so upsetting to some ministers and elders that Charteris had to face a barrage of criticism and opposition every time he sought the Assembly's blessing for his next move. His committee was denounced as inquisitorial, meddling and interfering; his ideas were laughed at, sneered at and ridiculed with all the sardonic wit of some of the best orators in the business.

Charteris' opponents were infuriated by his constant call for evangelism in the Church of Scotland. Evangelism was a nasty word among those who wanted the Church to jog along pretty much as it had always done. Evangelism was associated with the Free Church and the old sores of the Disruption. It smacked of emotional one-night revivals and was condemned as 'Plymouth Brethrenism', and Charteris himself was hotly criticised for sitting on platforms with Moody and Sankey and all sorts of 'volunteer' churchmen during the great revival campaigns of 1873 and 1881.

Charteris argued in response that the very popularity of these campaigns was proof positive that people were yearning for religious revival; it was up to the Kirk to keep that revival within the Church, by conducting its own evangelistic campaign wherever people lived and worked. No minister could do this on his own; the whole congregation must be rallied to help the minister. So he introduced deputies to go to the farm-workers and the fisherfolk, missionaries to tramp the Highlands during their summer holidays, and, through his Young Men's Guild, a whole army of part-time helpers eager and willing to march with their ministers into the backwoods of squalor in search of souls. For any minister who only wanted a quiet life visiting old ladies and polishing up a couple of sermons for Sunday, the sight of Professor Charteris rising to his feet in 1885 must have been distinctly disquieting.

This time he was intent on calling up the women. He had mentioned in many previous reports the sterling work being done by women, and the need to develop and organise them as an official working unit within the Church; now he wanted the General Assembly to give his committee the go-ahead to investigate the whole situation and come up with a specific plan for the next Assembly.

As he outlined his ideas for the most revolutionary of all his schemes, he stood as always on the right side of the Speaker's table, facing his packed audience. He was 50 years old now, thickset but still boyish-looking, with a good head of brown hair, slight whiskers tapering from ears to chin, bushy eyebrows and a fine Roman nose. His voice was firm and unhurried, but those who knew him well could tell that he was feeling nervous. As usual, the main counter-attack came from his two most regular antagonists, Dr Cunningham of Crieff and Dr Story of Roseneath. Dr Cunningham seized on a part of the report which told of mission work carried out in the East End of a city by a mothers' meeting of over 200: the minister of the parish had reported a striking number of 'confessed conversions and . . . changed lives', all due to the 'personal dealing with individuals by the ladies in charge and by myself'. Aha! said Dr Cunningham, Professor Charteris was clearly aping the methods of the Salvation Army and advocating 'female captains' in the Church of Scotland. Not to be outdone, Dr Story declared, to a round of applause, that there was no doubt that the tendency of the report was 'to bestow commendation upon what one might call somewhat irregular methods of religious operation'.

For impartial observers, it all seemed to be an occasion for much hilarity, according to *The Scotsman* editorial of 25 May 1885:

> No better comedy can be desired than the playing together of . . .
> Professor Charteris and Drs Cunningham and Story. The speeches and
> the dialogue are equally admirable. The joke about the brazenfaced
> female captains will keep the manse tables throughout the country in a
> roar for weeks together. The comic distress of the Professor, when Dr
> Cunningham marched across the House and convicted him from last
> year's report of an admiration for the 'female captains' which he had
> forgotten and denied, is also something to be remembered. Any one not
> familiar with the idiosyncracies of Presbyterian divines and the moral
> atmosphere of an Assembly would hardly go to hear a discussion upon

the 'Christian life and work' of the Church expecting a gay exhibition of wit and hilarity. But to Doctors of Divinity the methods of reclaiming a world lying in wickedness are capital subjects for wit and merriment. There is much humour in the contrast between the anxious gravity of the evangelising party, represented by Professor Charteris, earnestly but, it is to be feared, clumsily and unsuccessfully imitating revivalists and Salvationists, and the jolly contempt of the easy-going Moderates and Latitudinarians for all such 'striving after wind'. The sight of Dr Cunningham and Dr Story poking fun and hurling ridicule at Dr Charteris and his company going out by the hedge sides and trying to save souls by irregular methods, is immensely amusing; but there is food for serious reflection in the hankering of one party after evangelical salvationism and their admiring envy of the success of the Salvation Army, and in the exaltation by the other party of authority and respectability over the work of the saving of the lapsed masses.

It was a shrewd and sensible comment; and in the end it was the 'serious reflection' that won the day: when the laughter had died down and a vote was taken, the General Assembly gave Professor Charteris the authority he wanted 'to enquire into the subject of woman's work in the Church and bring up a definite report and suggestions for the next Assembly'.

The professor and his committee went about their task by the method they had pioneered for finding out what was going on and what people were thinking in the parishes: they sent out a questionnaire ('Queries', they called it) to every kirk session, inviting them to do the following:

(1) State what various forms of Christian work are being carried out in the parish by women.

(2) Offer any suggestions as to the best means of recognising and organising such work (a) parochially and (b) throughout the Church.

(3) Offer any suggestions as to the best means of making provision for the special training of women for various forms of Christian work.

In earlier years, many ministers had refused to respond to the committee's fact-finding exercises; but this time the replies came pouring in, and they proved what Charteris already knew well—that women were doing a vast amount of church work which was not officially recognised or formally organised, and that many, many more women were 'willing and eager to labour in home mission work if the Church would open for them a sphere of recognised usefulness'. All this went into the committee's next report to the General Assembly, along with the comments sent in by ministers and kirk sessions and all the evidence of women already at work, as fund-raisers for foreign missions, as Sunday school teachers, as sick visitors; as well as reports of women who were sewing for Zenana missions and Dorcas societies, delivering church magazines, or being called upon 'in special cases of distress'.

The replies all agreed that putting women to work on an official basis would be a tremendous shot in the arm for many a parish, and there were no hostile responses—although, presumably, the anti-women lobby merely ignored the 'Queries'.

A remarkable discovery was made from the replies: that there were no fewer than eight guilds, or associations of women church-workers, already in existence. One of these was in the tiny parish of Lintrathen, near Kirriemuir (the 'Thrums' of J M Barrie's *The Little Minister*). Lintrathen is now part of the linked parish of Glenisla, Kilty and Lintrathen, in Angus. It proudly reported to Professor Charteris' committee in 1885: 'Women work as Sunday School Teachers; do monthly visiting and tract distributing; work and collect money *etc*, for Presbytery Zenana Association. Each female worker has a district and the whole forms an Association under the Kirk Session'.

Even more interesting was the evidence, from the Kirk of St Nicholas in Aberdeen, of a woman's guild that was actually called that: the 'Guild of St Margaret in the Kirk of St Nicholas'. It took its name from Scotland's first woman saint, whose life is depicted in the stained glass windows of the church, and it had been founded in 1882 by the Revd James Cooper. Its proud motto was 'By love serve one another. Watch and pray'. St Margaret's is now incorporated into the Woman's Guild of the united North, East and West parishes of the Kirk of St Nicholas. It lays claim to being the oldest Woman's Guild in Scotland, and the one on which Professor Charteris based his own constitution for the Woman's Guild of the Church of Scotland. Certainly, Charteris must have been well acquainted with the affairs of St Nicholas Kirk —his wife had been a member of the West Parish before her marriage; and at the General Assembly of 1886, the Revd James Brebner of Forgue, in Buchan, speaking in support of Professor Charteris, cited St Margaret's as an example of how a woman's guild should work. (Indeed, at the very next meeting of St Margaret's Guild, the secretary was instructed to write and thank Mr Brebner for his remarks.)

The Guild's old minute books, carefully treasured down the years, show that the minister was the leader of the Guild, but was called the *Warden* rather than the president (an idea not taken up by Charteris), and that there was a sub-warden, a council, a secretary, treasurer and members—who were frequently referred to as 'sisters'. But they also hint at the tantalising possibility that St Margaret's may not have been the first guild after all. The Guild had a badge, and it is interesting to note that when its design was being discussed in 1882, 'A bronze badge of another Guild was exhibited at the meeting, and the chairman was authorised to make enquiries as to the cost of a similar one'. But no one now seems to know what this *other* Guild may have been.

While all the evidence was being sifted and summarised by the hard-working and unpaid Life and Work Committee[1], Professor Charteris was concentrating on that aspect of service which would be the pinnacle of his Woman's Guild—deaconesses. To have deaconesses in the Church of Scotland was his long-cherished dream, and the returns from the parishes indicated that many others would welcome the revival of the ancient Order of Deaconesses. Charteris knew its history inside out. He had often preached and lectured on the very first deaconess, Phoebe (Rom. 16:1–2, Authorised Version), 'which is a servant of the church which is at Cenchrea', holding her up as proof that St Paul himself had approved of women workers in the Church:

> I commend unto you Phebe our sister, which is a servant of the church which is at Cenchrea:
> That ye receive her in the Lord, as becometh saints, and that ye assist her in whatsoever business she hath need of you: for she hath been a succourer of many, and of myself also.

Charteris would also cite St Paul's advice to Timothy about the enrolling of widows into the sphere of church work (1 Timothy 5:9–10):

> Let not a widow be taken into the number under threescore years old, having been the wife of one man,
> Well reported of for good works; if she have brought up children, if she have lodged strangers, if she have washed the saints' feet, if she have relieved the afflicted, if she have diligently followed every good work.

No doubt his opponents would come right back at him with 1 Timothy 2:11–13:

> Let the woman learn in silence with all subjection.
> But I suffer not a woman to teach, nor to usurp authority over the man, but to be in silence.
> For Adam was first formed, then Eve.

Charteris would tell how Pliny, the Roman governor of Bithynia, had reported that he had put to the torture two women who were officially called deaconesses, in order to 'ascertain the truth' about Christianity. He would quote the beautiful form of prayer at the solemn service for the ordination of a deaconess, as prescribed in the so-called Apostolical Constitutions. He would refer to the existence of deaconesses at the Cathedral of St Sophia in Constantinople during the time of the golden-tongued St John Chrysostom in the fifth century, and tell how, 200 years later, the patriarch Cyriacus built a magnificent church in memory of his dead deaconess sister. To ill-founded charges of 'Popery!', Charteris would reply that deaconesses were not, like nuns, members of an exclusive community: a deaconess in the Church of Scotland would be an officer of the congregation, under the jurisdiction of the kirk session in the presbytery.

He had been researching all this material for years, in historical sources and on his travels abroad. He had made reports of his visits to institutions run by deaconesses in Germany, France and Switzerland, as well as the hospital served by deaconesses in Alexandria in Egypt. Now he set off with the Very Revd Dr John McMurtrie, editor of *Life and Work* magazine (1880–98), to inspect hospitals and orphanages and missions in England. They watched women at work in Dr Barnardo's Homes and in St Augustine's Orphanage of Mercy in London's Kilburn. They visited the London Bible-Women's Mission, and met all the deaconesses at the Manchester City Mission. At one such institution, at Mildmay, Charteris met a fine Scottish worker, Miss Katharine Davidson, and immediately booked her to be one of his first deaconesses.

The trip to England had crystallised his picture of the ideal woman to be a deaconess in the Church of Scotland: 'A trained worker who should combine the attributes of a capable sick-nurse and the highest type of Bible-woman'. He was now ready to face the 1886 General Assembly with a plan of action, and the unequivocal statement: 'The time has come for the formation of the Church of Scotland's Woman's Guild'.

The plan proposed three grades of service:

(1) A Woman's Guild open to all women who are engaged in the service of Christ in connection with the Church, and also to all who desire to be taught and trained to serve the Lord Jesus Christ.

(2) Within the Guild a higher grade called the Church of Scotland Woman-workers' Guild, consisting of Sunday school teachers, visitors, nurses, heads of Temperance Associations, and the senior members of congregations who have taken an active part in befriending the younger and less experienced female members and adherents; also those willing to serve, but unable to pledge themselves to regular and constant service.

(3) A still higher Grade of Deaconesses who would receive admission to that rank with the sanction of presbytery and after due training.

Once again the idea of women being recognised by the Church

occasioned much mirth, according to the report in *The Scotsman* on 26 May 1886:

> Mr J H Crawford, Abercorn, supported the deliverance. What possible reason, he asked, was there why the ladies should be relegated to the galleries, where they were then? (Great laughter.) It seemed to him that the time would come when the women would occupy the chair which the learned Moderator now so ably occupied—(more laughter)—and probably furnish him with a new chapter of its development in the history and dogma of the church. (Laughter.) He believed that many of our social evils would be removed by the healthy influence of female opinion. (Applause.)

Merrily or not, the General Assembly once again gave its approval, accepted the report as the basis for a comprehensive scheme, and authorised the committee to 'proceed prudently in accordance with it'.

Professor Charteris and his committee spent the summer and autumn drawing up the rules and regulations, which were then unanimously adopted by the General Assembly of 1887. They were printed in full in *Life and Work*, with the challenging plea from Charteris: 'Who will join this work?'

1. *Woman's Guild.*

1. The Association shall be called "THE CHURCH OF SCOTLAND WOMAN'S GUILD."

2. The general object of the Guild shall be to unite together all women who are engaged in the service of Christ in connection with the Church, or desire to give help to any practical Christian work in the parish, as well as all who are receiving Christian teaching and looking forward to Christian service.

3. Parochial branches, therefore, may take whatever form may seem most desirable to the minister and kirk-session for making a Parochial Union with the above-named object in view. It is intended that the members of Bible-classes, of young women's congregational associations, of mission working-parties or Dorcas societies, as well as tract distributors, Sabbath-school teachers, members of the church choir, and others similarly occupied, shall be incorporated in a branch, or in separate branches, and the members of such branches regarded as individual members of the Guild. Other workers might also, in special circumstances, be enrolled as individual members, though there were no branch of the Guild in the parish or congregation. (*Note.*—All members are requested to make the welfare of their fellow-members of the branch, and of the whole Guild, a subject of special prayer.)

2. *Woman-Workers' Guild.*

1. This Association shall be called "THE CHURCH OF SCOTLAND WOMAN-WORKERS' GUILD," and shall consist of experienced workers not less than twenty-one years of age.

2. Enrolment shall be made by authority of the kirk-session, after that court is satisfied of the member's Christian character and devotion to service for a period of not less than three years.

3. Such service may have been given in any department of practical Christian work in the parish, as, for example, in Sabbath-school teaching, or visiting, or nursing, or teaching a class, or promoting a temperance association, or in any mode of actively befriending younger or less experienced female members or adherents of the congregation.

4. Those who are willing to help, though unable to pledge themselves to regular or constant service, may be enrolled as *Associates*, upon their engaging to help by doing some work, or contributing some money every year. (*Note* 1.—Every member and associate is expected to use intercessory prayer for the Guild that it may accomplish its purpose, and for the members that they may make full use of their opportunities of service. *Note* 2.—Some of the members of this Guild might perhaps be able to go for short periods to assist ministers in organising the workers in their parishes. They are, of course, under no obligation to do this, but some would be glad and able to go on such errands of well-doing.)

3. *Deaconesses.*

1. Deaconesses, after their qualifications have been approved by the presbytery, shall be solemnly set apart by that court, at a religious service in Church.

2. There shall be an Institution or Home which shall be in connection with the Church of Scotland, and under the direction of the Christian Life and Work Committee, unless the General Assembly shall otherwise direct.

3. There will be two classes of deaconesses, equal in position, but having different spheres. (*a*) *Those whose qualifications have been attested by their work while residing in their own home.* (1) They shall have been known for not less than seven years as active workers, giving their life during that period very largely to Christian work. (2) They shall be free to work where they find themselves most useful in connection with the Church of Scotland, and subject to the minister and kirk-session of the parish. (3) It will be possible for those whose work has mainly been at home to reside for a time in the Institution, on conditions to be arranged, with a view to special training. (*b*) *Those who have been trained in the Institution.*—(1) They shall have been not less than two years connected with it on probation and in service. (2) If accepted as candidates, they shall during the first three months contribute £   for their own support; if thereafter taken as probationers, they shall, during their time of probation, be maintained in the Institution. (3) While being trained in it they shall be subject to the rules, and shall be prepared to go where sent for temporary service. (4) A limited number of those who have attained the grade of deaconess may remain in the Institution as their home, on conditions which shall be hereafter arranged.

Life and Work also printed a copy of the first Woman's Guild membership card.

The Woman's Guild was under way!

Note on Chapter 7

1 For years, the costs of the committee were paid out of privately raised funds, until the General Assembly authorised a budget financed by a twice-yearly church collection. When a poor collection caused the committee to overspend, Charteris would not go to the Assembly with a deficit, and he and

Mrs Charteris offered to pay off the difference; but the committee rallied round and raised the money from friends and supporters (with Charteris himself near the head of the list of contributors).

CHURCH OF SCOTLAND WOMAN'S GUILD.

Parish of _____

CARD OF MEMBERSHIP.

And pages 2 and 3 are—

PAGE 2.

"My soul doth magnify the Lord, and my spirit hath rejoiced in God my Saviour."
"Whose I am, and whom I serve."

———

THE MEMBERS OF THIS GUILD ARE UNITED TOGETHER WITH THE VIEW OF DEEPENING AND STRENGTHENING THEIR OWN RELIGIOUS LIFE AND OF PROMOTING GOOD WORKS; AND THEY RESOLVE:—

1. To give service to the Lord Jesus Christ as workers in His Church, or as receiving guidance and instruction with a view to work in future;
2. To meet together at such times as may be agreed upon;
3. To read a portion of Scripture and pray in private every day, and to go to church as regularly as possible;
4. In private prayer to pray often for the furtherance and success of the work undertaken by the Church of Christ, especially by the Church of Scotland;
5. To pray for the other Members of the Guild on Sunday morning, and on that day also to pray for a blessing on all the good works done in this parish, on the Parish Minister, and on all the workers.

———

"That they all may be one; as Thou, Father, art in me, and I in Thee, that they also may be one in us."
"Let the words of my mouth, and the meditation of my heart, be acceptable in Thy sight, O Lord, my strength, and my redeemer."

PAGE 3.

Member's Name _____

Address _____

Date _____

(Signed) _____
President.

8

Growing Up

A pyramid is usually built from the bottom upwards; but Professor Charteris had to start building his 'pyramid of woman's work' from the top downwards. This was because the bottom layer, the great foundation—the mass of women scattered throughout the length and breadth of Scotland who were to be the basis and main support of the Woman's Guild—was slow to get going. Women were simply not accustomed to forming committees and arranging meetings. They were not accustomed to starting anything, or belonging to anything, or doing anything, that had not been organised by men. This so-called 'Woman's Guild' had been thought up by men, approved by men, launched by men. The edict had gone out—'Organise the women!'; and the women sat and waited expectantly for the men to get things going.

And 'men', of course, meant the parish ministers. The next move was theirs, but many of them dragged their feet. Some heartily disapproved of the whole business; they did not want to organise women. Others feared that women would start organising *them*; they realised that once this thing got going, life would never be quite the same again, and they hoped that if they just hung back for a while all the excitement would die down and the whole business would quietly fade away.

But Professor Charteris had absolutely no intention of letting that happen. He had already prepared the ground before launching, first, the Young Men's and then the Woman's Guild. He knew that the most crucial factor in trying to rouse his weakened and demoralised old Kirk to new life and action was to get his ideas directly across to the people in the parishes. That was why he had started the *Life and Work* magazine, which had proved invaluable in whipping up enthusiasm for the Young Men's Guild. But a year after the inception of the Woman's Guild, its membership stood at only 2087 spread over 33 branches; and Professor Charteris used *Life and Work* to rally the ditherers and the faint-hearts:

There are nearly 200 ministers upon our Committee. . . . If each of those will set afoot a Guild in his parish, the thing is done. If, on the other hand, each of them wait to be implored, or encouraged, or dunned into taking such a step, I foresee nothing but weariness. . . . No doubt the thing will be done somehow, some day; but years—lives—may be meanwhile lost. I thus publicly beg my colleagues to consider the organisation of woman's work a trust committed to them by the Church we serve; a trust which they are bound in honour. . . to discharge to the very best of their ability. . . . I trust also that the women themselves will set about this new enterprise as the young men have set about their Guild. Will they take trouble, and arrange and organise and have it done at once?

If there be some ladies who do not understand how such social organisation is worked, let them come for a few weeks or months to our Training Home, and they will see that it is easy and effective.

The great thing is the Woman's Guild; all the rest will grow out of that.

The reference to 'our Training Home' was an indication that the top of the pyramid, at least, was functioning already. In 1887, as soon as the General Assembly had given its blessing to the whole project, Charteris had started looking for premises in which to train his deaconesses —resident students who would be doing a two year course of lectures and practical training for mission work at home and abroad. He wanted his 'Deaconess House' to be a home as well as a school for ministers' daughters and other well-bred young ladies who might be expected to take up the challenge of full-time service in the Church. The school was to be not too far from the centre of Edinburgh, so that the apprentice deaconesses could practise their missionary skills in one of the poor areas of the city. The first 'Deaconess House' was accordingly rented at 33 Mayfield Gardens in Edinburgh, where it opened its doors on 16 November 1887. (In the following year it moved to 41 George Square, before finally settling down at 27 George Square in 1890.)

Professor Charteris had already chosen the woman he wanted to run Deaconess House as early as 1886. She was Miss Alice Maxwell, youngest daughter of Sir William Maxwell of Cardoness, near Castle Douglas in Dumfriesshire. At first glance, she was an unlikely choice as superintendent of the first training institute for the first Order of Deaconesses in the Church of Scotland: she was only 30 years old, she had never been away from home, and she had never had any opportunity to study or even visit the kind of institution she would be required to run. Her health had never been robust; furthermore, in 1886 she had been physically exhausted after nursing her father throughout his final illness. She was not what people call a born leader; indeed, her sister described her character as 'always unassertive in spite of her capable businesslike mind'.[1] She was recommended to Charteris by her parish minister at Anwoth, and at first she had refused—although she was willing to go as a trainee or 'resident'. But Charteris was convinced that she was the right person for the job, and eventually she agreed to take it on—but only on condition that she was given 18 months in which to prepare herself, both physically and mentally.

So Alice Maxwell set off for a visit to Australia. Then she spent six months training with the deaconesses at Mildmay, at Rochester Deaconess Institution and at The Orphanage of Mercy in Kilburn, learning everything about the religious routine, the curriculum of lectures, and the various methods of 'working' a mission district. Meanwhile the Church of Scotland Deaconess House opened for business in Mayfield Gardens.

During Alice Maxwell's absence, the temporary superintendent was the young woman whom Charteris had 'poached' from Mildmay: Miss Katharine Helen Davidson, from Inchmarlo. She was as different from Alice Maxwell as chalk from cheese: healthy and robust in body and personality, a good speaker, a tireless worker, a graduate of Mildmay, a natural leader. One wonders why she had not been Charteris' first choice to run the Deaconess House.

The question of class may have entered into it, for there is no indication in the available records that Katharine Davidson was a member of the gentry. It is not so much that Charteris may have been a snob—but class was a fact of life in Victorian times, and much later too: in 1937, Annie S Swan wrote: 'I heard of a country lady not long ago who, from a platform, prefaced her remarks with these extraordinary words: "Ladies and Women!" '[2] To this day, many people think that a new venture, a fund-raising scheme, a charity, a business project, any new enterprise indeed, will have greater credibility, an aura of respectability, and a better chance of public support if it has a clutch of aristocratic titles gracing its letterheads. In 1887, people 'of quality' were expected to run things. It would be natural for Charteris to look for 'a lady' to supervise the Deaconesses who, being fairly well up the social scale themselves ('ladies of culture and position and intellectual power' was what was wanted, according to the Revd R Blair in *Life and Work*), could hardly be expected to take orders from someone who was their social inferior.

On the other hand, it could be that Charteris was simply an extremely shrewd judge of character, for Alice Maxwell turned out, against all the odds, to have been an inspired choice. From May 1888, when she took over Deaconess House, until she retired 23 years later, in poor health, half blind, and universally loved, she trained deaconesses and worked missions to the poor in Edinburgh with consummate

success. As for Katharine Davidson: after her stint as acting superintendent in Alice Maxwell's early absence, Charteris gave her a job as a
roving ambassador for the Guild, which lifted the Guild out of its earlier
inertia and made her something of a legend for resourcefulness and
sheer guts. After that she went on to make history as the first deaconess
to follow the herring fleet and minister to the fisher girls of Scotland.

Charteris would have liked to start the whole project with the 'setting
apart' of the woman he had chosen to be the first deaconess of the
Church of Scotland: the jewel in the crown, Lady Grisell Baillie. She
came into the category described in the Rules and Regulations as Class
A:

> Those whose qualifications have been attested by their work while
> residing in their own home . . . known for not less than seven years as
> active workers, giving their life during that period very largely to
> Christian work . . . free to work where they find themselves most useful
> in connection with the Church of Scotland.

This was Lady Grisell to a T. She was 65 years old when the Guild
started, and still giving her all in the parish of Bowden; but before she
could be put forward as the first deaconess, there was a hitch at the
autumn meeting of Edinburgh Presbytery, when a Dr Phin objected to
the idea of deaconesses being set apart by the presbytery: that would be
putting them above elders, who were ordained only by the kirk session,
a lower court than the presbytery. So the matter was taken to the 1888
General Assembly, which decided that 'setting apart' should be in the
hands of the kirk session.

It was 9 December 1888 before Lady Grisell was 'set apart' by the kirk
session of Bowden—an occasion which she affectionately called her
'wedding-day'; but, sadly, her beloved brother was not there to see it.
The Major had died on 29 September that year, and Lady Grisell wrote
to Professor Charteris (who was recovering in Italy from yet another
bout of illness):

> I think you will like to know that the people seem pleased with the
> honour conferred on me. They are taking it this way: that I am to be as far
> as I can be in my dear brother's place. To keep up his work and to prevent
> his influence among them . . . from fading away.

She went on to give Charteris a detailed account of the historic
ceremony in the little Border church:

> I stood in the centre of the church, alone all the time, just opposite the
> pulpit—the elders on each side. . . . First, the Session Clerk read all the

papers, every one, and the sentences from your rules. Then Dr A [her minister, 'dear, good, frail Dr Allardyce'] went up on to the steps of the pulpit, and put to me the three questions. I raised my head, looked him bravely in the face, and clearly and cheerfully said 'I do', 'I do', 'I do'. That was my moment of chief joy, as you will well understand. . . . After my answers Dr A pronounced the blessing, 'The Lord bless thee' (Numbers vi), and said I was now 'set apart'. He then went to the pulpit and addressed me, saying he would not enter on the duties of the office. 'You have been doing the work of a deaconess for many years'. He then besought me to strive to follow the example of my brother. He spoke very well, and everyone was touched. There was a full church, like on Sacrament Sunday. The dear Admiral, my brother, was much over-come.

When the first conference of the Woman's Guild was held in Edin-burgh in November 1891, Lady Grisell, DCS (Deaconess of the Church of Scotland), was accorded the honour of presiding at the morning session. Because of this, she has often been thought of by Guildswomen as the first president of the Guild; but in fact there was no question of a woman being a president of anything at that time. These were early days, and men were still in charge. Professor Charteris himself, or some other member of the Life and Work committee, started off every meeting, and it was not until the year 1935 that a woman presided over the Central Committee of the Guild for the very first time. At the 1891 conference, Alice Maxwell was allowed to take the chair at the after-noon session; but at the public meeting later that evening, the chair-man's address was given by a man, and resolutions were proposed and spoken to by seven men.

Various deaconesses and 'ladies', including Lady Grisell's sisters (Lady Aberdeen and Lady Polwarth) and her niece (Lady Balfour of Burleigh), sat in the chair of honour at subsequent meetings; but although Mrs Charteris was effectively doing the duties of a president right from the beginning, it was not until 1895 that the title of 'president' was attached to her name in a report.

Still, Lady Grisell was undoubtedly the Guild's leading light at that first conference in 1891. She was in her sixty-eighth year then, and alone in the world since her other brother, the Admiral, had died. She moved her audience in the Masonic Hall that morning to ecstasies of emotion with her clarion call to 'Go, work today in My vineyard'. Charteris' biographer wrote: 'None who were present ever forgot the sweet, pleading earnestness and the ringing musical voice that spoke with such winning, imploring attraction'. A young missionary dele-gate at the conference was quoted in *Life and Work* as saying, 'We

enjoyed the whole conference, but it was the holy beauty in the face of
the President that most of all impressed me'.

All this was said in sad hindsight; for after returning home to start a
branch of the Woman's Guild in Bowden, and writing to every branch
in the country urging all members to become total abstainers, Lady
Grisell caught influenza on her sick rounds. She died on 20 December
1891, only a month after her triumph in Edinburgh.

'There is sorrow on fair Tweedside,' wrote Professor Charteris in
Life and Work, wishing sadly 'that she had belonged to our Guild longer;
that it had been earlier in existence, to enlist her sympathies and receive
the impulse of her clear, bright spirit.'

So lived and died the First Lady of the Woman's Guild. The second
and the third to become deaconesses, Alice Maxwell and Katharine
Davidson, were 'set apart' together on 13 January 1889, in St Cuthbert's, the parish church of the poor and densely populated Pleasance
district of the Royal Mile, which had been chosen as the mission field
for Deaconess House. Charteris wrote to Alice Maxwell from Merano
in Italy: 'You are henceforth no solitary volunteer; you are on the staff
of the army.'

As a general who led from the front, Alice Maxwell combined her
duties as principal of the training house with daily forays into the slums
of the Pleasance, where she held kitchen prayer meetings, stair prayer
meetings, Sunday schools, mothers' meetings, even a fathers' Bible-
reading class. She visited the sick, reasoned with the drunks—and if a
woman could be persuaded to try to give up the demon drink, Alice
Maxwell would take her back to Deaconess House and look after her
while she endured what we nowadays call 'going cold turkey'—
suffering the terrible pangs of withdrawal from an addictive drug. The
delicately-reared baronet's daughter was doing instinctively what has
become a highly specialised area of medical care, and her experiences in
the Pleasance encouraged the Woman's Guild to make temperance
work an official part of their activities, and led to a remarkable bit of
pioneering social service in 1904 when a Guild cottage for the treatment of inebriate women was opened at Lasswade.

Alice Maxwell often had to cope with inebriate men as well as
women, but she and the deaconesses who followed her found protection from 'the rude word or coarse jest' in the deaconess uniform of
brown bonnet and cloak. The 'Brown Ladies', as they came to be
known, had safe passage in the Pleasance; but the younger student
deaconesses, or 'residents', who wore black dresses and black bonnets,
were only sent to carefully selected areas, and only after 'a few moments
of earnest prayer spent together in Miss Maxwell's room before they

started on their afternoon visiting'. Perhaps the most touching memory of Alice Maxwell's reign at Deaconess House is that she always kept the grass long in the garden there, so that the children she invited to parties and treats would have plenty of material with which to make daisy chains.

Those early deaconesses not only got no pay for the risks they took and the long hours they toiled both during and after training, but they actually paid for the privilege of living at Deaconess House. The cost was one pound a week (half-price for ministers' daughters); and even that was too much for some, as Professor Charteris pointed out in *Life and Work* in 1888:

> This is a time of pinching in Scottish manses, and even the small sum we ask from ministers' daughters may be beyond the power of many who in ordinary times would offer themselves. There are probably some friends and neighbours . . . who would be glad to give a young worker means of learning how to work.

Sponsoring missionaries for the foreign field was a popular idea. Many a Woman's Guild branch helped to pay the expenses of a local girl training for service abroad. On the very night that Miss Maxwell and Miss Davidson were being set apart in St Cuthbert's, a thousand Guildsmen were witnessing the ordination of the Revd John Graham as *their* sponsored missionary to Kalimpong. Sponsoring missionaries for the city slums of home, however, was a much less glamorous prospect; yet it could, and did, open the Diaconate, as the Order of Deaconesses is called, to other than those of private means. Not everyone could emulate the example of the Honourable Mary Scott, daughter of Lord Polwarth and grand-niece of Lady Grisell: she paid for her own training at Deaconess House before setting out in 1905 to serve for 50 years in India, wearing her brown deaconess dress in the heat and dust, without ever receiving a penny in salary, expenses or financial support from anywhere but her own family.

On the other hand, Miss Annabella ('Ella') Robertson, the youngest of 11 children of an Edinburgh railwayman, was able to enrol at Deaconess House in 1928 thanks to the sponsorship of the Girls' Guild, a junior arm of the Woman's Guild that was started in 1918. The girls paid Ella Robertson's £60-a-year board and tuition fees (she had given up her job as a seamstress, as well as her fiancé, to become a deaconess), and from 1931, when Ella donned the grey deaconess uniform (they were the Grey Sisters by then), the Girls' Association, as the young guildswomen were now called, paid her annual salary of £120 a year. For this handsome pittance she laboured in the slums of the Pleasance, amongst the prostitutes and model lodging-house inmates of Glasgow, and, after the Second World War, as the lone, pioneering missionary of the housing estates and resident deaconess to the vast, sprawling Colinton Mains housing scheme in Edinburgh. After a spell as deaconess at St David's Church, Viewforth, she retired at the age of 67, and at 95 was living in happy retirement in Liberton.

This is not a history of the Order of Deaconesses. But theirs is a proud story and no doubt one day the full story will be told, from the 'setting apart' of the very first deaconess to be trained at Deaconess House (Miss Mitchell in 1891) down to present times, when the Diaconate Board of the Church of Scotland runs a team of around 60 deaconesses, highly-trained professionals appointed mainly by the Department of Ministry and Mission to work with ministers in parishes of special need, such as large housing estates. Some are chaplains' assistants in hospitals and prisons and in the Royal Air Force; one is training officer at the YWCA in London; another lectures at St Colm's College in Edinburgh, where deaconesses are now trained; one is warden at the Sheltered Housing unit in Glasgow's Gorbals; one is part of the Community Ministry team in Glasgow's Drumchapel; one works for the Deaf Association in Dundee, another at the John Ross Memorial Church for the Deaf in Glasgow; some are secretaries on the Board of World Mission and Unity at the Church headquarters at 121 George Street, Edinburgh. Now, when women can become ministers in the Church of Scotland, many still choose to be deaconesses, and their role is still a unique one, serving every aspect of Church life, although no longer part of the Woman's Guild. But their beginning was inseparable from that of the Guild. Charteris used them to inspire the women in the parishes, to show the way and provide the work for willing, but slightly bewildered, hands to do.

Notes to Chapter 8

1   Mrs Horatio Macrae, *Alice Maxwell, Deaconess* (Hodder & Stoughton, 1919), p 46
2   Annie S Swan, *Seed Time and Harvest* (Nelson, 1937), pp 18–19

9

Mrs Charteris to the Fore

The first 33 branches of the Woman's Guild, as reported to the General Assembly in 1888, were:

Abbotshall, Kirkcaldy
Banchory-Tiernan, Kincardine
Banff
Barony, Glasgow, Woman Workers' Guild
Barony, Glasgow, Young Women's Guild
Caddonfoot, Selkirk
Dalreoch, Dumbarton
Dunnichen, Forfar
Dunning, Perthshire
East, Aberdeen (probably the East parish of St Nicholas)
Evie and Rendall, Orkney
Forgue, Buchan
Grahamston, Falkirk
Greyfriars, Aberdeen
Greyfriars, Edinburgh
Holburn, Aberdeen
Kelso, Roxburghshire
Kilmarnock
Kirkmahoe, Dumfries
Manor, Peebles
Montrose
Mordington, Duns
Newington, Edinburgh
New Rothesay, Bute
Penninghame, Newton Stewart
Prinlaws, Leslie, Fife
Renton, Dumbarton

Rosemount, Aberdeen
St Bernard's, Edinburgh
St Columba, London
Sorn, Ayrshire
Tolbooth, Edinburgh
West Linton, Peeblesshire

Some of the new Guilds could only claim members working as Sunday school teachers; others were running a Bible class; some were singing in church choirs; others were sewing for the zenanas, or distributing the Church magazine; one gathered its membership from women running a local branch of the YWCA.

To St Columba's Church of Scotland in Pont Street, London, goes the honour of having started the first Woman's Guild in England. It beat to the starting-post the oldest Scots kirk in London, the Crown Court Church—or the Kirk of the Crown of Scotland, as it was known when it opened in 1719. There had been a Scottish Embassy in London long before the Union of the Crowns in 1603; it was at the north end of Whitehall, with a palace, a mansion house and a chapel. This was where the Scots worshipped who followed King James VI to London in 1603 when he became James I of England. The chapel was destroyed in 1698 and money was raised by private subscription to build the first Crown Court Church in its place. That building was replaced by another in 1909. Meanwhile, in 1884, Scots living in a more residential part of London opened a new Church of Scotland—St Columba's in Pont Street—and three years later started a branch of the Woman's Guild there. When St Columba's was destroyed by enemy action in 1941, the Guild worked tirelessly to help raise the money to build the new church.

The old Crown Court Church was three years behind St Columba's in starting a Guild, but once it got going, in 1890, it was everything Professor Charteris could have wished for: bursting with energy and enthusiasm, full of ideas—and right from the start, run entirely by women. It was the first Guild to have a woman as its president: Lady Victoria Campbell, granddaughter of Queen Victoria, daughter of Princess Louise and the 9th Duke of Argyll. She and her sister, Lady Frances Balfour, who succeeded her as president, were two very modern-minded ladies with strong ideas about women's emancipation; being the dedicated church workers that they were, they saw the Woman's Guild as not only a force for strengthening the Scots Church in London, but also as an opportunity to get women up and doing and taking a lead in life. And this was 18 years before Emmeline Pankhurst founded the suffragette movement in 1905! With Miss Alice Grant, who was Secretary and Treasurer for 50 years, Lady Victoria soon had a large Sunday school organised with 400 pupils and a mothers' meeting 200-strong. The Guild held a huge fund-raising sale every year for nearly 100 years (except in wartime), and during the First World War they darned all the socks of the wounded soldiers in Endell Street Hospital—some 250 pairs a week. They contributed handsomely to Kalimpong Hospital, and adopted a child at Kikuyu Hospital in Kenya.

But besides all the knitting and sewing, Sunday schools, prayer meetings and sales of work that were part and parcel of every new Guild, St Columba's in Pont Street was probably unique in holding, right from the start, regular meetings with no other purpose than to let women hear eminent speakers talking about subjects of topical and philosophical interest—a privilege that had always been reserved for men, and which had been denied to the girls who wanted to attend the Gabbing School in Wamphray. Scots writer Annie S Swan, a staunch member of the Church of Scotland as well as being a popular author of romantic novels, went down to London to address the St Columba's Guild on 'The Racial Differences between the Scots and English'.

As well as running the London Guild for 23 years, Lady Victoria started up guilds in her native land, in the Campbell country of Argyll. She always said that one day, when she was looking out of the ruined windows of Iona Cathedral, she got the call to go and minister to the islanders of Tiree and the Ross of Mull. She spent her summers trekking the hills and glens, recruiting those who were too remote to attend Guild meetings, calling them home-workers whom she banded into a Fellow-Workers' Union. She wrote reports to Professor Charteris beginning 'Dear Professor Pax' and signed 'Your affectionate Highland child'. She addressed annual Guild conferences. She wrote articles in *Life and Work* deploring women's working conditions—'thousands of women are working ten, twelve, and even fourteen hours a day at wages ranging from four to seven shillings a week'—and urged those who were thinking of emigrating to travel under the protection of the British Women's Emigration Association, of which she was the Scottish representative. But she steadfastly refused to become a Deaconess, even though Professor Charteris was keen that she should.

After the two London churches, Newcastle was the next English guild. Today, there are ten Church of Scotland parishes in the Presbytery of England; and among these, there is a Woman's Guild branch in Gillingham, in Liverpool, in Aldershot, and two in Corby (St Andrew's and St Ninian's). Corby is known as the 'little Scotland' that was settled by steelworkers who emigrated there with Stewart & Lloyds in 1934.

Back in Scotland in 1888, Professor Charteris had been far from satisfied with the progress of the Woman's Guild in its first year. He said so in no uncertain terms in *Life and Work*; he also appointed a committee of fourteen men and three women to get things moving. They visited manses all over the country, trying to persuade ministers and their wives to start Guilds; and their efforts resulted in the formation of a number of new branches. But the catalyst that really woke the parishes up was Katharine Helen Davidson, the third deaconess. As soon as the arrival of Alice Maxwell released her from her temporary post as superintendent of Deaconess House, Katharine Davidson was appointed an Honorary Deputy and sent out into the highways and byways of Scotland, carrying the fiery cross of the Woman's Guild. Bright, lively, never at a loss for something to say, she addressed audiences in churches, church halls, village halls and manse parlours all over Scotland. Travelling by pony and cart she visited 100 parishes in one year, between 1889 and 1890. When she reported to the first conference in 1891, the number of Guild branches had risen to 113, with 8371 members.

By then, Katharine Davidson was already ploughing new ground. In 1890, Professor Charteris had sent her to Glasgow to open a small Deaconess House at 5 Berkeley Terrace, where the residents were allowed to attend lectures at the Royal Infirmary and train as nurses in the wards (the Royal Infirmary in Edinburgh was giving similar facilities to the girls training in the parent House). But it soon became obvious that the strain of nursing in a big city hospital, and doing mission work as well, was too much for the girls. Besides, they were preparing for a life that would involve administering basic nursing in city slums and country cottages, or in small hospitals in the Himalayas or the African bush, and it was felt that training in a large infirmary was not really appropriate. Professor Charteris decided that the Guild should have its own hospital, and started a fund to build one in the Pleasance beside the new Mission premises that were opened in 1891. St Ninian's Mission House, as it was called, had cost £3000, all raised by private subscription. It housed the Sunday schools and the mothers' meetings, and the girls' club, and the Sunday services; but it was also meant as the central premises of the Guild, and its first occasion was a welcoming meeting for the delegates to the first conference of the Guild in 1891.

At this point, Mrs Charteris comes into the picture. She had always been there, working behind the scenes, running mothers' meetings, organising missions. Tributes to Mrs Charteris always gave her the highest accolade accorded by Victorians to good and faithful wives: she was 'a true yoke-fellow and loving helpmeet'. Accustomed as she was to listening to mawkish sentimentality, she must have squirmed at 'true yoke-fellow and loving helpmeet'. It simply did not adequately describe Katie Anderson Charteris. Good and faithful wife she certainly was; but she was also a down-to-earth, no-nonsense, independent person in her own right. She was unconventional, impatient of male pomposity (a national disease in Victorian times), and always poking gentle fun at her husband's titles as he climbed the establishment ladder: professor, chaplain to Queen Victoria and King Edward VII, Moderator of the General Assembly, Dean of the Thistle, and Doctor of Divinity twice over (Edinburgh and Aberdeen). Her keen, practical mind was behind many of the best things the Guild did in its early years, and she excelled at translating her husband's heady schemes into practical terms that would involve the lowliest member in the remotest parish.

In 1891, Mrs Charteris was made editor of the new Woman's Guild supplement in *Life and Work*, and suddenly the Guild came to life for thousands of women who had found it difficult to appreciate the importance of the little bits and pieces they were doing in their own small corner. Mrs Charteris opened up the whole picture for them with racy reports from headquarters, on-the-spot descriptions of life in Kalimpong and Poona, and news from far-flung branches. Ideas were exchanged, hints and criticisms offered, appeals for help were made directly instead of having to be fed laboriously down from General Assembly to presbytery to parish minister to Guild.

Guildswomen rushed to tear the sheets off their beds and rip them into strips for bandages after Deaconess Katharine Davidson, following the herring fleet from the Orkneys and Shetland to every herring-port in Scotland and south to Yarmouth, had given an eye-witness account of bandaging the cut hands of the fisher girls, preparing comfortable billets for them, and holding packed Sunday services for fishermen and girls. (A long line of courageous churchwomen was to follow Katharine Davidson in the work among the fisher-folk—in particular, Deaconess Ella Ross, who went from serving 13 years in the Glasgow Lodging House Mission to 10 years in the fishing ports. When she died at Largs in 1986, an old Peterhead fisherman wrote to deaconess headquarters in Edinburgh: 'Ella Ross came amongst the fisher-folk of the East, North East and North West of Scotland whilst they were at their work, to minister to them, supply to their needs, spiritually and physically. The fisher-folk took Ella Ross to their hearts . . .').

Mrs Graham, wife of the Men's Guild missionary at Kalimpong, appealed to the Woman's Guild to build a cottage hospital at Kalimpong and send out a lady doctor to take charge of it. Later, Mrs Charteris printed a letter from her husband, apologising because the Life and Work Committee had been unable to find a woman doctor: 'We have advertised everywhere, and we have inquired . . . in and beyond the United Kingdom and. . . we can find no one. In a few years some of those women who are now medical students may come to our help; meanwhile they are not ready'. So a man was sent instead, a former tea-planter called Dr Ponder. He arrived in 1893—'the first missionary of the Woman's Guild. . . . Our first desire was to send a woman. . . . Now we are constrained to see that God has done for us what is far better'.

Katharine Davidson reported on the funeral of a 22 year old fishergirl from Stornoway called Mary McLeod, who had gone back to work at the herring-gutting too soon after contracting measles. She had died in her lodgings without doctor or minister, with only a Gaelic Bible-woman at hand. All the fisher-girls were at the funeral in their shawls, weeping. An elder of the Gaelic church gave out, line by line, the 90th Psalm, sung in Gaelic. When the men left for the cemetery the Mission ladies held a prayer meeting for the women, and the Bible-woman read from her Gaelic Bible an account of Lazarus' resurrection.

Stobhill Woman's and Young Men's Guilds held their annual picnic together, and spent a most enjoyable day amongst the hills.

Mrs Charteris asked women to send in suggestions for the design of a Woman's Guild badge, 'by which one member might recognise another and take advantage of their common ground on which to meet, without awaiting introductions' (even Mrs Charteris seemed as if she had swallowed a dictionary on occasions). The badge was ready in 1893, price ten-pence or, as a pendant, nine-pence. It was small and lozenge-shaped, in red, white, blue and gold. The colours were symbolic: the red of the St Andrew's Cross in the centre stood for sacrifice and service; blue was for loyalty to the Master, the congregation and the Guild movement; white was for purity of motive; and the gold encircling band symbolised 'the chain of prayerful fellowship binding all the members of the Guild together'. The badge has been a big seller down the years. Guildswomen still wear it proudly and, like kilted Scots abroad, or men wearing the old school tie, they greet perfect strangers like long lost friends—or, as Mrs Charteris put it, 'take advantage of their common ground on which to meet, without awaiting introductions'.

The year of the badge, 1893, was also the year in which the ambitious

Guild scheme to bring country produce to the poor of the cities really got under way. Warehouses were rented as Country Produce Stores (in Edinburgh it was at 8 Dalrymple St), and Mrs Charteris gave a vivid account of the scenes there every Saturday morning when the railway van arrived with the weekly supplies. Everywhere there were hampers of eggs, cauliflowers, cabbages, turnips, rhubarb, blackcurrants. Masses of flowers filled the street with fragrance and colour—heather to gladden a Highlandwoman's heart, white flowers for a grave perhaps —and all at a fraction of what the cost in a shop would have been. It was a triumph of energy and organisation, as the carefully-packed hampers were despatched from tiny village stations all over Scotland and delivered by rail with unfailing regularity and punctuality to the cities.

The country members were unstinting in their gifts to the Country Produce Stores, and to the Gift Depot where all kinds of donated goods were sold in aid of Mission. But some country members complained that they seemed to be the only ones who were doing the giving: one wrote, 'Why shouldn't townsfolk give presents in kind? Our goods cost us time, work and money, too, just as their goods cost them'. And a town shopkeeper objected that sales of gifted goods at bargain prices were taking the money out of the tills of shopkeepers: 'Is it right to sell them for the benefit of missions to the heathen?'

Mrs Charteris would have none of that sort of argument. And she took to task the attitude of some people towards helping the poor:

> Some earnest people think that well-to-do Christians should be very sparing in their efforts to bring the poor *temporal* comfort. They dread that in trying to succour dejected minds or lonely hearts, or shivering, hungry bodies, we shall be pauperising them, preventing the drunkard from feeling the consequences of his misconduct, and so forth. . . . Careless alms-giving may, and does, pauperise, but generous, considerate brotherly kindness is a different thing . . . Surely we are to do good to *all men*, not just the *deserving poor*?

She challenged the patronising do-gooder:

> Our Master said explicitly, 'When thou makest a feast, call not thy friends and thy kinsmen, but call the poor, the maimed, the blind.' But when we make a feast we *do* call our friends and do *not* call the poor. Once in a way some rich people give them a day's pleasuring; but for the most part all we, who are neither poor nor rich, do for those who have fewer earthly comforts than ourselves, is to club together to give them a 'mission tea' at Christmas, or a brief excursion at midsummer. . . .
>
> How easy it would be for most of us to become acquainted with a few poor families, and then do all we can to be really *friendly* with them. . . .
>
> If we only send the city missionary to the mourner, and direct the

Dr and Mrs Charteris   *(source: Hodder & Stoughton)*

Wamphray Parish Church

Lady Polwarth, President 1907–20

Lady Grisell Baill
(source: Hodder & Stoughton

Deaconess Alice Maxwell
(source: Hodder & Stoughton)

The Kalimpong Mission Buildings
(source: Hodder & Stoughton)

Mary Lamond
President 1920–32

The Woman's Guild Branch Secretaries' Conference 1935

A Woman's Guild Assembly in the Usher Hall

Photograph by courtesy of 'The Glasgow Herald

Lizzie Buist Meredith, President 1932–39
Elizabeth McKerrow, 1943–47

Allison Lyon Harvey, President 1939–43
Anne Sutherland (formerly Mrs Jacobs), 1947–51

Lois Jarvis, President 1951–54

Ailsa Miller (2nd from left), President 1954

Jessie Dingwall
President 1955–59

Grace Hay
President 1959–63

Isabel Douglas
President 1963–66

Kathleen Grieve, President 1966–69

Elizabeth Anderson, President 1969–72

Maidie Hart
President 1972–75

Mary Millican
President 1975–78

Daphne MacNab
President 1978–81

Anne Hepburn
President 1981–84

May Smith
President 1984–87

Dr Archibald Hamilton Charteris
(source: Hodder & Stoughton)

Mamie Magnusson, author

wanderer to the nearest poorhouse, and give a clothing ticket to him who
pines with piercing cold, the task will not have at all the same effect. . . .

One of the brightest things in our Guild Supplement is the testimony it
gives that in farmhouses, manses and mansions in the country, as well as
in the towns, friendly gatherings of poor and rich are growing more
general. . . .

It is not giving alms that is wanted; it is giving friendship—friendship
real and hearty.

It must all have sounded pretty strong to an audience that was fairly
well-off in the main, and so steeped in class consciousness that it was
almost unconscious of it. Month after month, Mrs Charteris' busy pen
made them sit up in manses and mansions, town houses and country
manors. And right bravely they rose to the challenge—even if some of
their ideas of self-sacrifice might sound faintly ludicrous to a more
egalitarian society. One lady suggested a cut in her dress allowance as a
way of helping to raise funds at a time of particular crisis for the Church
in the foreign mission field:

> Is not self-denial in the matter of dress a duty at this crisis? Let every
> Guildswoman who has not already denied herself in this respect, calcu-
> late her expenditure for the last five years, and deduct a tenth part from
> the yearly average. The one half of this she might devote to the proposed
> Blantyre Self-Denial Fund . . . and the other half to some cause such as
> the Guild Home Mission in Pleasance.
>
> A less costly fur cloak or silk mantle, a dress less extensively trimmed,
> rather plainer underclothing, a pair or two of gloves the fewer, would not
> make so very much difference to the individual. . . . And may I further
> suggest that their contributions should be signed by merely the initials of
> the givers, or by some *nom de plume*, so as not to let the left hand know
> what the right hand doeth.

Mrs Charteris quoted a woman speaker at the second biennial
conference of the Guild, in Glasgow in 1893, who had appealed to 'Girls
of Leisure—girls who are exempt from the necessity of earning a
livelihood':

> No one would wish our girls to give up all their ordinary amusements,
> pack away their paint-boxes, lock their pianos, hang up their tennis-
> racquets for ever in the hall . . . but let them learn to think of others
> beside themselves. . . .
>
> One way in which girls of leisure may do good work is by making
> friends with working girls, and helping them to spend their hours of
> freedom in a way that will do them good. . . . Let our girls find a
> pleasure in sharing their pleasures with their toiling sisters, and let not the
> objection be raised that working girls should be kept in their proper

place. . . . Why should ease and idleness and needless luxury be the rule for the wealthy and fashionable, and grinding, unvaried toil be the portion of the poor?

Almost overnight the Woman's Guild was changing people's attitudes, stirring people's consciences, opening people's eyes to glaring inequalities and rousing women to look critically at conventional social habits and behaviour—but not in any overtly political sense. Most of these women, including Mrs Charteris herself, would have shuddered at the thought that they were often voicing exactly the same sentiments as the rabble-rousers who supported the new socialist movement. They were merely putting Christian principles into practice—as Professor Charteris had known they would—with a fervour and enthusiasm that left many of their menfolk breathless. And in so doing they were finding their voice. The long 'seelence' was over, and women tumbled over themselves in their eagerness to express themselves in print and on platform.

Sometimes they got completely carried away, like dear Miss McInroy, first of a heroic line of devoted Guild secretaries, who tied herself in knots over peas and pods at the 1893 conference:

> We may compare the Woman's Guild to a pea-vine, on which each parish branch of the Guild is a pod, and the various sections of work in that branch are the peas. A good many of us are apt to think that the parish branch of the Guild is only another pea . . . but it is really meant to be a pod, enclosing all the various peas, each quite distinct, but all united by *their* pod, and through it to the main stem. There is no need to point out that the pod in no way challenges comparison with the peas! Its function is different; its worth is in its capability of keeping the peas together and encouraging their growth; its glory is in their health, size and number.

1893 was also the year that the Woman's Guild got its official 'Hymn of the Woman's Guild'. Few if any of today's Guildswomen have ever heard of it; fewer still know that the Guild has actually had *two* hymns, not one. The first was written by Charteris himself, according to his biographer:

> The Woman's Guild hymn, beginning with the line 'By the hopes we deeply cherish', was written by Dr Charteris from the text [(RSV) Psalm 68, v.11]—'The Lord giveth the Word: the women that publish the tidings are a great host'. This was set to music by the late A L Peace, Mus. Doc., to the tune called 'Phoebe'.[1]

Unfortunately, neither the text nor the tune of this first attempt seems to have survived—simply because in the event they did not catch on. Charteris and Dr Peace (who was associated with Glasgow Cathedral and was musical editor of the *Scottish Hymnal*) had collaborated earlier on an extremely successful hymn for the Young Men's Guild. Dr Peace had composed a tune called 'Guild', and Dr Charteris had written the words while convalescing on the shores of Lake Merano in Italy. It was first sung at the Young Men's Dundee conference in 1889, and was an immediate success:

Believing fathers oft have told
What things by God were done. . . .

finishing with the rousing refrain:

Like brothers, true, of one accord,
To hold one faith, to serve one Lord.

The words and the music caught perfectly the rousing spirit of an army on the march, and when sung by a mass of male voices it was tremendously moving, in tune with the joyous, evangelical, militant hymns that were coming into the Church via the mission halls and the influence of Moody and Sankey and the Salvation Army. The hymn 'Believing Fathers' went first into the *Christian Endeavour Hymnal*, and then was included as No. 259 in the Church of Scotland *Hymnary* compiled in 1897, and as No. 521 in the *Revised Edition* of 1927. Sadly, it was dropped from the *Third Edition* published in 1974, although more martial favourites like 'Onward Christian Soldiers' and 'Stand Up, Stand Up for Jesus' were retained. Perhaps it was the constant call to 'brothers' and a specific reference in one verse to the Guild (Young Men's) long since disbanded, which made the text feel out-dated; but a few word-changes might have allowed a grand tune, and yet another example of the Charteris influence on church tradition, to remain in the repertoire.

Charteris, on his own admission, was not a natural hymn-writer (his original version of 'Believing Fathers' had to undergo some changes before it was accepted for the 1897 *Hymnary*), but this initial success seems to have inspired him to try his hand again, this time for the Woman's Guild, with Dr Peace as his musical collaborator. Unfortunately, it seems that the rousing melody of the original 'Guild' tune for the Young Men's Guild was much more of a hit with the ladies than the tune 'Phoebe' that Dr Peace now composed especially for the Woman's Guild. So the Woman's Guild decided to use the 'Guild' tune again, and a new hymn was written to it by the Revd Dr J Elder Cumming, then of Newington Church in Edinburgh, later of Sandyford, Glasgow. It was published in the April issue of the *Guild Supplement* to *Life and Work*:

HYMN OF THE WOMAN'S GUILD

1   O Christ the Lord! who died for me,
Teach me to know Thy will,
That from Thyself I too may learn
How best to serve thee still
In daily life and hearty work
At home, abroad, where 'er
Thou callest me to follow Thee:
Be this my only care!
And thus we too, with one accord,
May minister to Christ the Lord!

2   Once, Lord, in holy Galilee
Where walked Thy blessed feet
The women followed in the way,
Or hastened Thee to meet.
They ministered to Thee, and now
I find an open door;
For she still giveth to the Lord
Who giveth to the poor;
And thus we, too, with one accord
May minister to Christ the Lord!

But this version never reached the official hymn books, and never really caught on. Today it is all but forgotten. As part of the centenary celebrations, a competition was launched to find a new hymn for the Woman's Guild; it will be fascinating to see if it catches the imagination better than the two earlier efforts of nearly a century ago.

Note to Chapter 9

1   Arthur Gordon, *The Life of Archibald Hamilton Charteris* (Hodder & Stoughton, 1913), p 369

10

The Dream Fulfilled

Two new hospitals were built in 1894, the one in India and the other in Edinburgh; and the Woman's Guild took on the responsibility of entirely maintaining the one, and continuously supporting the other.

At Kalimpong, the Eastern Himalayan mission run by the Young Men's own missionary, Dr Graham, and his wife, the women paid for all the medical work. They paid for the medical missionary, Dr Ponder. They paid for the building of the mission hospital (the Charteris Hospital, as it was named), and all its furnishings and equipment. They paid for its upkeep, and provided comforts and little luxuries for its patients down the years.

For Charteris, this nurturing of mission work abroad by the women at home had always been a major personal ideal. His early passion for foreign ministry, instilled in him by his mother, had never been diluted by the passage of the years or by the weight of his own responsibilities. His heart was always with the missionaries. He cared about them, worried about them, felt concern for them. He wrote to them all personally, and personally received their reports as convener of the Life and Work Committee. After 1894, when he retired as convener, he continued to write to them and they to him; and when they were on furlough they would always come and visit him and Mrs Charteris at their Edinburgh home, Cameron House. (The old house, which used to be on the southern outskirts of Edinburgh, is now firmly part of the suburbs; in 1973 it was converted into flats as part of a modern development in Cameron House Road, Newington).

Mrs Charteris listened avidly to their stories, and then passed on their requests in the *Guild Supplement* in such a way that the needs of the foreign mission reached the women in the parishes not just as yet another request for money but as a personal appeal that involved them closely with the individual missionaries and their Indian friends, helpers, patients and pupils: real people, with names and even (when the Guild had bought Dr Ponder's sister a camera) faces.

When the walls of the new hospital were almost complete, Dr Ponder sent a list of requirements that took up quite a space in the *Guild Supplement*:

22	large-sized beds about 75″ by 30″—iron
4	cots for children
36	pairs red blankets, 'good quality'
48	pairs white sheets to suit bedsteads
12	pairs white sheets to suit cots
12	binding blankets
12	dozen pillow slips
12	pewter bed-pans
24	enamel basins, 14″ diameter
36	enamel cups for drinking tea
36	urine glasses
24	dozen towels, cheap, for Natives
4	dozen towels better quality
8	waterproof sheets, 54″ by 36″
4	Hanging Lamps to light Rooms of 16ft square
18	Small wall lamps
6	Hurricane lamps
1	good Filter
	Ticking sufficient to make Mattresses and Pillows for beds
1	Rubber Stamp (for linen marking)

The Guild went into furious action, purchasing bales of cloth, cutting it, distributing it, sewing, sewing, sewing, in weekly work parties from the Orkneys to London. At these sewing marathons the workers would be entertained by songs and recitations from members of the company, or sometimes the minister would read from an 'improving' book while the needles flew. All kinds of garments were made for sale at bazaars and garden fêtes to raise money for the equipment that had to be bought for Kalimpong. All kinds of ingenious ideas were thought up to make money. Country children were asked to forgo their breakfast egg and bring it to school for sale at a town bazaar. Mayfield Guild in Edinburgh started another idea that became very popular as a fund-raiser: the accumulator. Twenty-four members of the Guild were each given a penny, and three months to put it—and themselves—to work. One woman used her penny to buy an empty cream jar, which she painted and then sold for sixpence; with the sixpence she bought a doll, which she then dressed and sold for a shilling; with the shilling she bought an old pair of bellows for 6½d and some ribbons for 5½d, then painted the bellows and decorated them with ribbons, and sold the result for 2/6d. At the end of the three months, the original two shillings handed out in pennies to Mayfield Guild had become £2 10s.

The work never stopped, because the demand never ceased. As soon as one carefully waterproofed and sun-proofed box had been despatched on the high seas to India, another was being packed with the latest requests. 'The largest size of box went out to Kalimpong in time for Christmas,' Mrs Charteris reported. It was packed with 'pretty holland bed-covers', towels, sheets and sleeping-suits from St Columba's in London, West Kirk in Greenock, Dunfermline Abbey, Melrose, Pollockshields, Auldearn, Newington and the Pleasance.

Side by side with this item of news there was another call from Kalimpong:

> The ordinary Lepcha or Nepali have, as a rule, only one suit of clothes —that which they carry on their backs; so our friends at home can imagine what this means when in sickness they are laid up for any length of time. . . . We should be most grateful for any help in this way. We would suggest nightgowns of various sizes, suitable either for men or women, and little ones, of course, for the children. . . . We find often, too, that patients on going out have not got warm clothing to put on, and a jacket or under-vest, or warm cloth for a skirt-like arrangement which the women adapt, would be of great benefit. . . .

The best idea of all was getting Guild branches to 'adopt' their own beds in the Kalimpong Hospital, paying ten pounds a year for each bed and the nursing of the patient in it, and providing all the bedding, clothing and comforts for its occupants during the year. The parish or district paying for a bed had its name inscribed on a panel above the bed, and doctors and nurses from Scotland felt it a link with home to treat patients high in the Himalayas in beds labelled 'Pollockshields', 'Pleasance', 'Perth', 'Kippen', 'Wishaw', and other well kent place-names all the way from Shetland to London.

It was a time of tremendous enthusiasm and of giving, in terms of labour, goods, money and service, on a scale never before seen in the Kirk. Women were showing an ability at fund-raising which surprised and delighted the men of the Church, but which has paradoxically proved an irritant to many Guildswomen down the years, who felt that the men considered them good enough for nothing else in church life than fund-raising—and tea-making. Yet women who had never in their lives managed more than a housemaid, or a tea-party on the lawn, were now organising markets and bazaars, handling and banking large sums of money, buying cloth in bulk, despatching goods abroad, holding meetings, appointing committees.

It was exciting. It was fun. It was Live Aid and Band Aid and Oxfam combined, operating a hundred years before its time. It was doing good. It was feeling good. It was faith in action, love at work—and the women enjoyed every minute of it. The hallmark of the Woman's Guild of the Church of Scotland—their inimitable and indefatigable capacity for doing the Lord's work and having a whale of a time doing it—was created in those heady years of helping sick Indians in the mission at Kalimpong. They honoured their commitment in varying ways down the years. As the demands on the women's time and talents increased and the Church became more and more dependent on the Guild to finance its projects, no request from Kalimpong was ever turned down. The Guild built a house for Dr Ponder, for instance. The Girls' High School, like the hospital, was a special Guild responsibility from the day it was started by Dr and Mrs Graham. In 1937 the Guild paid for the remodelling and enlarging of the school hostel, and the electrification of the compound. Later they built an extension to the Nurses Home, and sent money to modernise the maternity department of the hospital. In more recent years they were paying for cement to thwart white ants attacking the junior school hostel at Kalimpong.

There were those, of course, both inside and outside the Church, who frowned on foreign missions. They felt that Kalimpong's plea on behalf of Indians who 'as a rule, had only one suit of clothes', ignored the fact that there were plenty of deprived folk in Scotland's cities who had only rags to wear, plenty of children going barefoot in the Scottish winter, and all of them hungry. Charity begins at home, was the cry. But the Woman's Guild was working hard on *all* fronts. Home Missions were a high priority also—just as much as Kalimpong—and the reports from deaconesses beavering away in slums and freezing fishing stations were a constant reminder of how the other half was living here in Scotland, and of the needs and comforts that the Guild was expected to provide.

Mrs Charteris started a system of Guild 'marriages' ('alliances' as they were later called), with branches in remote districts joining up with city branches and helping each other in whatever way they could. The town parish would be supplied with fresh country produce to distribute in the slums of its districts, while in return the town might visit country members in city hospitals, or send items in short supply in the country. For many years, children in city slums and Children's Homes around the country were regularly supplied with warm jerseys and hats and gloves knitted by Guild partners in Shetland. Skelmorlie in Bute 'married' St Paul's in Glasgow, and sent '48 garments of good serviceable material, beautifully made, no impossible buttonholes or "anything-will-do" saving, but the best of shaping and stitching with tucks to let down'.

Elgin Guild started an Industrial Class: 'a small effort to brighten, help, and, if possible, raise the lives of a few hard-working mill and factory girls. One of its objects is to give them a liking for sewing and knitting, *etc.*'

Mayfield in Edinburgh invited all the domestic servants and shop-girls who were members of the church to tea in the hall of St Ninian's Mission in the Pleasance, by kind permission of Dr Charteris, who 'honoured the gathering by being present'. After tea the minister spoke of the relative duties of mistresses and servants, and of how each could 'conduce to the welfare and happiness of the other by mutual interest and forbearance. . . . Music, songs and recitations followed and Dr Charteris then spoke of the dignity of service and invited all servants present to become members of the Guild. This a good many did'.

Rubislaw in Aberdeen followed up this idea, and gave their domestic servants not only tea, music and song, but a series of *tableux vivants*. A 'considerable number' enrolled themselves as members of the Guild and signed on to do some work for the Ladies' Working Party. Aberdeen East put a Dorcas Table in the church where everyone attending the annual meeting of the Guild could deposit a garment for the poor.

But the biggest event on the home front for the Guild in 1894 was the opening, just four months after the Kalimpong Hospital, of the Deaconess Hospital in the Pleasance in Edinburgh. It was named the Lady Grisell Baillie Hospital but always known as the Deaconess Hospital, and it was built for the poor of the district: the inscription above the door read— *To Christ in His Poor*. This was Dr Charteris' dream-child and the joy of his heart. He had pleaded for it, begged for it, put his own money first on the subscription list, lovingly supervised every stage of its construction, and persuaded his doctor to let him postpone his latest convalescence in Italy in order to be present at the opening of what his biographer called 'the only hospital of any Protestant Church in Christendom' (with the sole exception of a hospital run by the Waldensian Church). The opening was performed by Lady Grisell's brother-in-law, Lord Polwarth, and the hospital was accepted in the name of the Church of Scotland by the man who had given Charteris such a hard time when he was trying to promote the idea of the Guild at the General Assembly—that year's Moderator, the Right Revd Dr Story. In his own speech at the opening, Charteris said that he had been shocked to learn that owing to unforeseen costs the building budget had been overspent by £200; but he disclosed that he had already been handed

£100, and he said he was sure that the other £100 would come in before the ceremony was over. During tea in the mission hall after the opening, he came rushing in with his face wreathed in smiles and his hands full of banknotes totalling £130: the new hospital would start not just free of debt, but with a surplus.

It was small and private and homely, with softly tinted walls, large bright windows, and comfortable beds equipped with the clever new invalid tables that could be moved up and down the bed. There were basket chairs, a Bible and a hymn book at every bedside, and flowers everywhere.

At first there were only two wards with 22 beds and two cots, some of them gifted by individuals in memory of relatives, and others maintained by congregations. The matron was Miss Ella Pirrie (later to be made a deaconess), who had trained under Florence Nightingale and worked in hospitals in Germany and Ireland. She had three staff nurses and seven probationers to help her to run the new hospital at first. But the accommodation soon had to be enlarged to 40 beds, and a Nurses' Home built for 15 nurses and probationers. The new beds were financed by donations or endowments, and in one year 264 branches of the Woman's Guild sent contributions. In 1937, to celebrate its Jubilee, the Guild endowed a small ward in the Deaconess Hospital which became known as the Guild Ward. For years they supplied bed linen, nightgowns, eggs, fruit, vegetables, flowers and any other comforts the patients required. After the matron's death the Guild, in tribute to her memory, founded the 'Ella Pirrie Linen League' – a great network of sewing and mending and laundering to keep the bed linen in the Guild Ward in good condition.

As the hospital's reputation spread, patients were sent from outside the area, and Mrs Charteris had to print information about how it worked, and what the conditions of entry were:

> Beds are quite free, and are for patients that can be treated in hospital, either surgically or medically.
>
> We . . . do not take cases of consumption, or diseases that are incurable, as we could fill our beds at any time with these and nothing else.
>
> Any patients from the country wishing admittance should obtain a letter from their own doctor stating the nature of the case; also a recommendation from the Parish Minister or Guild Secretary.
>
> Town patients should apply personally at the hospital any morning at 10 o'clock when the doctors are in attendance.
>
> It is not by any means necessary that patients should be members of the Church of Scotland. We have had all creeds in our wards: Jews, Roman Catholics and Salvationists. . . .

Since opening two years ago we have had over 500 patients, coming to us from all parts of Scotland. . . .

We would like to thank the many Guild-friends for money and gifts in kind. Many have sent old and new clothing, enabling us to send patients out warmly clad who had come to us in rags. Some sent game, wine, eggs, fruit, vegetables, jam and flowers. . . .

One little lad came to the hospital from the Cowgate. The father had deserted the mother and two children, neither of whom could walk. She tried to support them by making lace at night and selling it in the day—sometimes making as much as 10d, out of which she had to pay 7d for a bed for the family; the remainder was for the family's food.

Anecdotes like that brought in even more donations from the good-hearted *Guild Supplement* readers: Mrs Charteris reported a gift of £1000 to endow a bed for old men, in memory of the donor's father.

By 1910 it would cost £1350 to endow a bed in perpetuity at the Deaconess Hospital; a cot in the children's ward could be endowed for £700. The average cost of maintaining a bed for a year was £52. The average number of beds occupied per day was over 35, and the average length of stay of each patient was 24 days. More than 1700 out-patients received surgical treatment at the hospital that year, attending 5648 times, while nurses paid 3160 visits to people in their homes—130 of them maternity cases. The annual cost of running the hospital was £2400. The Deaconess Hospital is now part of the National Health Service.

When the first official Health Visitors were appointed in Edinburgh in 1908, the Town Council accepted the offer of voluntary help to carry out the compulsory visitation of all infants, in accordance with the 1907 Births Act. As the city was already divided into church districts, the new Voluntary Health Visitors Department asked the churches to appoint representatives to report on babies in each district. Miss Maxwell, the superintendent of Deaconess House, organised the St Ninian's district and did much of the visiting herself. She also did all the secretarial work, receiving the fortnightly reports from the other Visitors and filling in the forms for the Public Health Department, as well as attending fortnightly meetings in the City Chambers—and all this while she was running Deaconess House and the mission in the Pleasance. Miss Maxwell continued to do voluntary public health work for some time after her retirement through ill-health in 1911.

The Guild took on another responsibility in 1898 when the Robertson Orphanage, founded by Dr William Robertson of Greyfriars, was taken over by the Life and Work Committee to be run by the deaconesses. Here was yet another call on the Guild's goodwill: 21 little

girls to be fed and clothed, dolls to be dressed; rooms to be brightened
with flowers; and gifts to be sent for birthdays and Christmas. Mrs
Charteris kept the needs of the orphanage before the Guild at every
opportunity, and was a frequent visitor herself. She loved children,
although, sadly, she had none of her own; indeed, she and her husband
had all but adopted their nephew, Archibald Hamilton Charteris, who
lived with them for ten years, and once wrote to his uncle: 'Of all uncles
who ever stepped, you surely are the best!' Perhaps it was in caring for
this boy, whom circumstances had temporarily separated from his
parents, that Mrs Charteris found herself caring about the children of
the missionaries serving all over the world. Few missionaries could
afford boarding school fees, and unless there were relatives willing to
take them in, the children had to be left with strangers, perhaps only a
landlady, to see to their schooling, their comfort, their health, and their
moral and spiritual well-being.

Mrs Charteris longed to start a home for missionaries' children. She
broached the subject at the 1897 Guild conference in Edinburgh, and
then in the *Guild Supplement*, where Professor Charteris also added his
support:

> Parents and children of the Scottish Church, will you try to make a home
> for these children? . . . The idea of the projected home is not that of a
> charity. We propose to offer a Scottish home for about the same outlay as
> would be needed for them in the unbroken family on the mission field.
> We build this castle in the air near a great city, with lots of bedrooms
> where little cots may be stretched. Beside it may be a field where the
> children can play, and where their own cows graze; big trees where their
> swings could be hung; an old garden where each wee thing might have its
> own plot to work in and 'keep and dress it', sometimes sowing seeds and
> tending plants that father has sent home—and yet near some of the
> schools where instruction is to be had both cheap and good.

The money for a Home-House came pouring in, to the tune of
£3395—a quarter of it donated by the professor and his wife. They
found just the right house, in 1900, with the right kind of old-fashioned
garden, in the little country village of Duddingston, near Edinburgh,
and two ready-made 'aunties' to take charge of it: Miss Minnie
Paterson, an ex-missionary in India, and her sister Miss Maggie.
Miss Minnie served at the Home-House (which later moved to
Musselburgh) for 37 years, and Professor and Mrs Charteris played to
the end of their days grandfather and grandmother to the children.
Every one of the 50 children had a turn of spending a long weekend with
them at Cameron House or, later, their retirement home in Peebles.
'The Guild Mother', as they called Mrs Charteris, was a frequent visitor

at the Home-House. She knew every single child by name, and every Christmas she sent half-a-crown in an envelope for each Christmas stocking in the Home-House. Later, she changed it to postal orders for the older children. She wrote to the 'aunties': 'I was greatly hurried in sending off to you the children's postal orders. I remember how I used to enjoy Christmas shopping. So I hope they will also be able to get some fun out of spending my small gift . . .'

In another letter, she wrote: 'Your bairns are here, and it is making me almost young again, hearing of all their happy chatter . . .'

And again: 'It is very nice to be looking forward to seeing you all, and I do hope we shall have a fine day. You will be at Peebles station at 11.30 *am* where some of us will be meeting you. I think the best plan will be for us to walk up, so that you will all see Peebles. And then we will make the bus come up to fetch you all in the evening . . .'

When the parents of one girl wanted her back with them in India, Mrs Charteris wrote to Miss Minnie: 'I never realised how much I would feel parting with the child, and I know Aunt Maggie and you will be feeling just the same. . . . Those were just like our very own children. The child is young, but it is her dear home and her native land she is going to, and I don't wonder they could not bear the idea of educating her for some work in this country, when it seems now so probable their home will always be in India . . .'

And when an epidemic of influenza was raging: 'I am so grieved about the bairns, though I know the high temperature is natural in children. Dear wee Rosie! I trust she is better by now. Give her a dear kiss from me . . .'.

It is difficult for us to appreciate just how much time and trouble were involved at the turn of the century in taking as concerned an interest as Mrs Charteris did in the Home-House. There was no lifting of the telephone to make a quick enquiry. Everything had to be done by letter, or in person. Typewriters were still a new-fangled invention. All the Charteris letters to missionaries and to Guild leaders, all the requests for support and for funds, all the letters of encouragement to new Guilds and new deaconesses, all the regular contributions to the *Guild Supplement*—they were all written out by hand. By the end of the century even Mrs Charteris was beginning to tire, and in 1901 she resigned as editor of the *Supplement*. Her husband had retired from the university in 1898, and in the following year Edinburgh made him an honorary Doctor of Divinity. He was now Dr Charteris—and would be doubly so in 1906 when Aberdeen conferred on him the same honour.

In 1902 they gave up their house in Edinburgh and moved to

Kingswood, a lovely mansion on the edge of the King's Muir, near Peebles. This was to remove Dr Charteris a little distance from the temptation of too much work in Edinburgh. He was still striving to find some means of re-uniting the separate factions of the Church. The union of the United Presbyterians and the Free Church in 1900 was only a tantalising foretaste of what might be if men could be persuaded to give a little here and a little there for the greater good of all. Despite an alarming deterioration in his health, Charteris was always ready to speak at meetings up and down the country, to travel to London, or to take part in private discussions with representatives of the United Free Church, in the hope of finding the solution that even the end of patronage in 1874 had failed to achieve.

Kingswood in Peebles was to be his semi-retirement, and at the same time provide an opportunity for Mrs Charteris to nurse her deaconess sister, Helen Anderson, who was now worn out and prematurely aged by the strain of working for many years among the women prisoners in Calton jail. The little family was hardly settled into Kingswood, however, before doctors diagnosed that Dr Charteris was suffering from a malignant tumour and gave him only three months to live. As a last resort he was persuaded to go to Glasgow and try 'the new X-ray treatment'. Within a couple of months he was writing to a friend in Aberdeen: 'You may have heard that the X-rays have had a marvellous —almost miraculous—effect upon me. My general health is quite renewed. My malady is arrested . . . I was in the valley of the shadow, and had no fear or uneasiness. I wonder if I shall be able to use my so-far-restored health?'

And use it he did, to complete one last chapter of his Guild dream. He wanted a Rest House for his deaconesses, a place where they could spend a holiday or a convalescence, a place to which missionaries could return from foreign fields, a retirement home for women who had given up their own homes to serve the Church. Dr Charteris had been promoting this idea for a number of years, and some money had been sent to him for that purpose, including £200 from the Life and Work Committee and £500 from his sister-in-law, Helen Anderson. Now he determined to push ahead with the scheme, and Mrs Charteris made an appeal for help in a letter to Guildswomen in the *Supplement* in 1906. She signed it 'Your affectionate old President', for she had just resigned as president of the Woman's Guild in April of that year.

That year, too, they sold the house in Wamphray that Dr Charteris had built for his mother and sister, who were both now dead; and most of the furniture went to the new Rest House, which was opened at Appin Lodge in Eskbank in 1907.

In April, 1908, when Dr Charteris was 73 years old and, as he put it, 'aging at the rate of three years per annum', he and Mrs Charteris were staying overnight in Edinburgh on their way back to Peebles from a visit to Bridge of Allan. He was sitting in a chair in their favourite boarding-house in Melville Street that evening when, without warning, he took a stroke and died instantly.

He was buried in Wamphray kirkyard, not far from the graves of his parents and his brother and sister. Mrs Charteris went back to live in Edinburgh, in Salisbury Place, where she continued to play host to the children of the Mission and the Home-House, and sorted out her husband's voluminous papers for the official biography that was being written by the Honourable Arthur Gordon. When it was published in 1912 she sent a copy of it to every Woman's Guild branch in the country—765 of them by then.

Mrs Charteris died on 18 November 1918, 7 days after the end of the First World War. She was buried beside her husband, and their gravestone proclaims her, 'The First President of the Women's Guild of the Church of Scotland'. It is an inscription that makes every pilgrim Guildswoman wince at the mis-spelling; for Dr Charteris had always insisted on calling it the *Woman's* Guild—never *Women's*.

Mrs Charteris left a bequest of £300 to build a Guildroom for Wamphray Church, and it was opened and dedicated in 1928. Wamphray Church was linked with Moffat in 1971, and the last Guild meeting was held in the Charteris Room in 1974. Meetings were held for another three years at the Old Manse in the village; and then, in 1978, Wamphray Woman's Guild was wound up.

New Directions

With the resignation of Mrs Charteris from the presidency of the Woman's Guild in 1906, and the death of Professor Charteris himself in 1908, the first major chapter of the Guild story had come to an end, some 20 years after it came into being. But there was no break in continuity. Mrs Charteris became honorary president, and was succeeded as national president by the Honourable Mrs Scott of Humbie, wife of the Master of Polwarth who was a nephew of Lady Grisell Baillie (Mrs Scott later became Lady Polwarth when her husband succeeded to the family title).

The Guild was in tremendous heart. By 1906 there were 675 branches with 47 143 members, and the numbers were still rising steadily. The two major commitments of the early years—the hospital and school at Kalimpong, and the Deaconess Hospital in Edinburgh—were flourishing, nurtured by a constant stream of funds and gifts from members of the Guild.

But change—immense change—was on the horizon. The serene social certainties of the Victorian Age (despite the fearful social inequalities), and the bright optimism of the Edwardian Age, were about to disintegrate in the welter of world war. The Woman's Guild would have to adapt its thinking to suit changed circumstances, to find new areas of need. Enterprises that the Woman's Guild had pioneered in its early days would be absorbed into larger institutions. The twentieth century would bring the Woman's Guild immense new challenges, new roles to define. The one thing that no one, however visionary, could have predicted was the astonishing speed and scale of the changes that lay ahead: not just the Woman's Guild, but women themselves, would never be the same again. One thing remained constant, however —the Guild's belief that the world was full of people in need of help, both at home and abroad, and that it was the Guild's duty and privilege to provide help in every way it possibly could.

One of the central tenets of belief, not surprisingly, concerned the significance and sanctity of the home. As early as 1891 the Guild had launched a Mothers' Union movement: 'By uniting mothers for conference, prayer and sympathy it seeks to elevate and purify the life of our Scottish Homes and protect them against grave and manifest evil'. But curiously enough this Guild initiative never achieved the spectacular success of some other Guild enterprises. Perhaps this was because there was already in existence another, mainly Episcopalian, Scottish Mothers' Union, and the Guild was chary of seeming to set up a rival 'opposition' movement. A compromise was reached (a slightly uneasy compromise, one suspects) whereby the Guild Mothers' Union would not form a separate branch in areas where there was already a SMU in existence; instead, Guild members were to join the SMU with a special membership card marked 'Church of Scotland Woman's Guild'. As a result, the movement never really took off within the Guild. Nevertheless, there were 83 branches in existence in 1930; but in that year, the Scottish Mothers' Union became incorporated under the Board of Trade and was given a new constitution, and this brought matters to a head. The new governing body of the SMU had no room for representatives from the Woman's Guild; and so, in 1931, the Woman's Guild formally severed its connection with the SMU and decided to revert to its original intentions and carry on its work for and with mothers as a special section of the Guild itself.

In the course of the 1930s a considerable number of members left the SMU to form a breakaway group called the Scottish League of Wives and Mothers. There was now talk that there should be a union between this League and the Guild Mothers' Union; but there was a division of opinion within the Guild about the wisdom of such an arrangement, and no definite decision was reached. It was not until the early years of the Second World War, under the determined presidency of Miss Allison Harvey, that the Woman's Guild tackled the dilemma head-on. In 1942, when the number of Mothers' Union branches had dwindled to 52, the Guild held a Conference on Home Life. It reiterated the importance of religious instruction for the young, and the need for systematic visiting of homes; but the fundamental decision was to dissolve the Guild Mothers' Union. The 1943 Guild stated:

> The work formerly undertaken by the Guild Mothers' Union has this year become an integral part of Guild activity, as it was recognised that the important task of helping the home to make its Christian contribution to the New World must be no extra, but the very foundation of Christian reconstruction.

In her private, unpublished memoirs, Allison Harvey summarised her views on this momentous step:

> There was a fairly large remnant of the Scottish Mothers' Union that now sought union with the Guild mothers. It called itself the Scottish League of Wives and Mothers. On the Guild Central and Executive Committees there was a strong division of opinion. Not being either a wife or mother (no fault of mine) I still held strong views, and my view was that it would be disastrous to draw away our young wives and mothers' groups with an interdenominational body. So I, and fairly big support behind me, moved that we form our own within-Guild branches where possible, but at least attached to Church of Scotland congregations. This won the day. . . . In this case, as I look today at the Young Wives and Mothers' Groups, I feel we did the right thing, because they are our hope for the future.[1]

A Home Life Sub-Committee was set up 'to bring before Councils and Branches the importance of getting in touch with young mothers'. It was the start of something that was to tax the Guild's policy-makers right down to the present day, as will be discussed in a later chapter —the effort to integrate the young with the old in the Guild, to reconcile the interests of young mothers, working mothers, young wives and young women in general, and to attract them to the Guild in the face of the countless other opportunities for public service and social enjoyment open to women in the second half of the twentieth century.

The problems that had faced the Guild at the beginning of the century, when Lady Polwarth was president, had been rather different. In those days an afternoon at the Mothers' Union was a thrill beyond compare for women tied to home and children for seven relentless days a week. In the city slums, home life was often so appalling that the weekly mothers' meeting was a woman's only escape from the constant struggle to keep her family clothed and fed. The situation was exacerbated by the availability of cheap drink. Drunken husbands refused to let their wives attend meetings, or abused them when they returned, deriding their efforts 'to elevate and purify the life of their Scottish Homes'. Some women just gave up and took to drink themselves. It was the attendant misery caused by drink, encountered by deaconesses and guildswomen in their city mission, that inspired the Guild's Temperance Movement. As early as 1890 a Guild conference in Dundee had formally adopted Temperance as part of the work of the Guild. Lady Grisell Baillie's last act before her death in 1891 had been to send a letter to branches asking them to join the fight against strong drink. In 1894 the first meeting of the newly-formed Provincial Council resolved to 'ascertain the number of total abstainers in each branch', and in 1897, at the request of the Women's Temperance Association, the Woman's Guild agreed to assist more directly and actively in 'this great cause which has become a national concern'.

By 1902 it was reported that Guild branches had started putting up Refreshment Tents at country fairs and Highland Games to provide tea and food in opposition to the usual beer tents. This was such a success that in 1903 the Titwood branch in Glasgow raised the money to buy a large tent of their own, which they handed over to the Guild to be hired out to other branches at a small charge. Local Guildswomen rallied round to provide the refreshments wherever the tent happened to be, first at the St Boswells' Cattle Show, then on to Kinross and Auldearn for country fairs, then Crossmichael and Stranraer. It proved such a draw that other tents were purchased, and the Guild Tent became a crowd-puller at every big open-air event all over the country. The quality and quantity of food served was tremendously impressive; no wonder it was so popular! At one Highland Agricultural Show the Guildswomen served, among other items, 1500 pounds of beef, 270 pounds of salmon, 170 pounds of butter, 1500 pounds of strawberries, and a quarter of a ton of sugar.[2] The takings of £631 more than covered the expenses, but the labour involved was a measure of the enthusiasm of those early Guildswomen and set the standard for the Guild's reputation for top-class catering.

It was at the 1903 conference in London (the first to be held furth of Scotland) that a plan was enthusiastically launched for a Guild 'Retreat' for 'the care and treatment of inebriate women'. A small house with accommodation for seven women was opened in Polmont the following year, and was exchanged in 1910 for a larger one at Esktower, Lasswade, with room for 12–15 women. It was named the Guild Cottage, maintained by the contributions of Guildswomen, run by the Temperance and Guild Cottage Sub-Committee, and had a deaconess and former Guild secretary, Miss Margaret Johnston, as its superintendent. At this time a powerful temperance lobby was calling on the government to legislate for the compulsory removal of alcoholics ('the inebriated', as they were then called) to places of treatment; and the experiment at Guild Cottage, albeit amateur and unscientific but based on the experience of women like Deaconess Alice Maxwell in the slums of the Pleasance, was considered so important that in 1909 the Temperance and Guild Cottage Sub-Committee was asked to give evidence before a government committee that was preparing the Inebriates (Scotland) Act. The Guild reported that 62 women (46 of them married) had been admitted to the Cottage since 1904. Of these, 17 remained for less than three months, having proved 'unsuitable'.

Nine were still under treatment. Of the remaining 36 who had completed the full 12 months' residence, 14 were doing well, 6 were much improved, and 16 were 'not traceable'.

One barrier to persuading women to take treatment at the Guild Cottage was that they were expected to pay for part of their keep there, so in 1911 the Guild decided to provide an extra £50–£60 of income so that all patients could stay there free of charge.

With the outbreak of war in 1914, there was an immediate increase in drinking among men, especially in camps and barracks. The authorities were suitably alarmed: 'We are fighting Germany, Austria and Drink,' a cabinet minister was quoted as saying, 'and as far as I can see, the greatest of these deadly foes is Drink'. Guild leaders urged their members to join the League of Honour for Women and Girls of the Empire which was pledged 'to abstain from all alcoholic drink during the war'. They sent a petition to the General Assembly 'praying them to urge Lord Kitchener and the Secretary of State for Scotland to employ the legislation available for lessening the temptation that surrounds men in barracks'.

The temperance lobby was calling for full Prohibition. The government refused to go that far, but made drastic changes in the liquor laws in 1915 with an amendment to the Defence of the Realm Act, making it illegal to drink before noon, or to take part in 'treating' (which obliged a man in a party of five to buy five drinks instead of one—'standing his round'), or to buy drink on credit.

The Guild opened a second Guild Cottage, at 24 Broughton Place, Edinburgh, in 1915, in anticipation of a spate of wartime drink victims; but the strange thing was that while men were drinking more, drinking among women began to decrease. Or perhaps it was not so strange after all: men had plenty of cause to want to deaden their feelings in that terrible war, but their drinking was done away from home, and many women knew peace for the first time in their married lives, as well as the freedom to run their homes as they wanted and the luxury of a regular income from the few shillings a week they were allotted from their husbands' service pay. In the event, the new Guild Cottage was never fully used. The old one at Lasswade became run down. Superintendent Margaret Johnston went off to do war work, and the Guild Central Committee appealed to the membership for 'strong, willing girls' to go to Lasswade and put the cottage garden in order. By 1916 the cottage was being used to give rest and care to married women with children they could not leave, and in 1918 when the war ended the Guild Cottage was finally closed.

Peacetime or no, the Guild continued to wage its war against drink, and in 1924 its temperance work was gathered into a new organisation, the Women's Association for Temperance. This was strengthened at the union of the Churches in 1929 by the United Free Manse Ladies' Total Abstinence Society, and became the fourth of the Guild's four major committees, known to generations of Guildswomen as the WJM, the WFM, the WHM and the WTA—the Women's Jewish Mission, Women's Foreign Mission, Women's Home Mission, and Women's Temperance Association (later to become the Women's Temperance and Morals Committee, which was to run a club for girls in Edinburgh in the 1950s and '60s).

Over succeeding years, as the women's committees became part of larger units of the Kirk's work and witness, Temperance became the responsibility of the Board of Social Responsibility, but Guildswomen continued to respond generously to any appeal in the cause of Temperance. In 1977 they raised £21 716 to help the Social Responsibility department provide workshop centres for recovering alcoholics.

When the First World War broke out, the Woman's Guild had 777 branches and 57 131 members. The membership, in fact, had been rising rapidly, largely due to the efforts of deaconesses and other volunteer deputies going round the country starting new branches and whipping up support. The first 'official' deputy (a polite way of saying that she was paid) was Miss Agnes Simpson, an indefatigable attender of meetings in far places in all weathers; she was only prevented from boarding the train to Fort William at 5 *am* one snowy morning by a determined guard who told her: 'My orders is—no perishable goods beyond Crianlarich!' Jessie Rettie was another intrepid deputy who made perilous journeys by land and sea in a systematic visitation of the branches, starting in Orkney and Shetland and working her way south, taking in places like Islay and Gigha in the Western Isles. She visited no fewer than 100 branches in 1911; and in the following year the growing Guild raised enough money to buy a pulpit and stalls for the Charteris Memorial Church, which was opened during Assembly week in 1912.

The 1914–18 War was a time of tremendous activity for Guildswomen. At first, like all the other women in the country, they stayed at home knitting socks and sewing pyjamas for the fighting men, but as the war progressed women started going to work in the munitions factories, as tram conductors, farm-workers and nurses. They joined the Women's Royal Army Corps and the Women's Royal Naval Service. Many Guildswomen were posted abroad on war service: the Woman's Guild of St Columba, Oban, for instance, sent food and comforts to three of their members who were serving with the Scottish

Women's Red Cross Unit in Serbia. The Guild raised £3000 to provide huts and canteens for servicemen and women, first at Turnberry and Crail, then Dreghorn and Cupar. There were two Guild centres for women in Edinburgh, and the Guild gave grants to help local efforts at Fort George.

The 1918 Guild report said:

> Club and canteen leaders have established a bond of affection between girls and the Guild, and the Guild look forward to the establishment of hostels and clubs for young women in great centres of population to bend them to the Church, and lead them into service for God.

Indeed, St Margaret's Hostel for women and girls was opened by the Guild in 1919 at 10 Park Terrace, Glasgow, and Lister House on Edinburgh's Mound was rented as a hostel for 50 business girls and students. These were highly significant signs of the times. In the midst of its busy end-of-war activities (which, typically, included making 1000 surplus Army kilts into clothes for children in Europe), the Guild was hard at work preparing for the changes that would face it when the war was over. The biggest change of all was in women themselves. They had shown that they could do all kinds of jobs that would never have been contemplated before the war. They had taken charge while the men were away fighting. They had bobbed their hair and shortened their skirts as they rolled up their sleeves. They were driving cars and even aeroplanes. They had won the right to vote: for women over 30 in 1918, soon for all women over 21. The Guild's answer to the new situation was to form the *Girls' Guild* in 1918 for young women from 15 to 30. For many years there had been *Junior Guilds* in many branches, taking girls as young as ten years old, but there was no equivalent to the *Girls' Auxiliary* of the United Free Church which was a lively organisation of young women in their twenties and late teens which had started up in 1901 to support foreign missions and then gone on to be involved in a wide range of social interests (unemployment, housing, temperance, education) as well as providing their Church with an enthusiastic supply of Sunday School teachers and Girl Guide captains. They were devoted Church members, strong on evangelism, with leaders who were experienced in raising money, running competitions, leading prayers, and speaking in public.

The older girls and young women of the Church of Scotland were eager to have an organisation like the Girls' Auxiliary in their own Church. They were already sharing summer schools for missionary education, evangelistic campaigns and experiments in Sunday school teaching with the United Free girls. The men of the two Churches were taking a long time to settle their differences; but as early as 1914, the Woman's Guild had accepted a proposal from the women of the United Free Church to set up a joint committee 'to consider methods of co-operation in mission and evangelical work'. The contacts that followed made the Church of Scotland girls even more determined to have an organisation of their own.

The Woman's Guild held a conference in June 1916 to consider 'the Relationship of the Girlhood of the Church to the Woman's Guild'; and there they resolved 'to make fuller provision within the membership of the Woman's Guild than exists at present for the girlhood of the Church, possibly on the lines of the Girls' Auxiliary of the United Free Church'.

In 1917 the Guild began revising its Constitution to include a new section of the Guild for girls from 15 upwards 'who may, if they so desire, remain members till they reach the age of 30'. A conference was held in November to put the scheme for a Girls' Guild to the girls of the Church, and to suggest the areas of service they might cover: missions of the Church at home and abroad, 'needs arising out of the war', social and temperance work, and help with the Junior Guild. The Girls' Guild was accordingly launched in 1918, and by the following year it had 60 branches with 2000 members. In their first year the girls raised £200 to build a hostel in India, and in 1923 they adopted their first missionary, Dr Toni Scott, in China. The girls' missionary zeal was further strengthened by the absorption into their ranks of the old Fellow-Workers' Union, a band of young enthusiasts that had been founded by Charteris and recruited by Lady Victoria Campbell to support the missionary efforts of the Woman's Guild.

The Girls' Guild adopted another missionary, paid for the training of Parish Sisters, bought a car for the Kikuyu Mission in Kenya, helped at children's play centres, gave concerts, took part in services at lodging house missions and became 'aunties' to the girls in the orphanage at Musselburgh. They published their own magazine, *The Trailmaker*. And when the two great Churches eventually united in 1929, the Girls' Guild and the Girls' Auxiliary slipped easily into union as the Girls' Association. It survived until 1961 when it celebrated its diamond jubilee (based on the date of the foundation of the Girls' Auxiliary), and then formally disbanded.

The revisions that had to be made in the Woman's Guild Constitution to accommodate the new Girls' Guild also included a simplification of the conditions of membership that had been laid down by Dr Charteris. They now read:

Membership in the Woman's Guild implies undertaking some definite
act of Christian Service, taking God's Word as the rule of life, cultivating
the regular habits of prayer and faithful attendance at Divine Ordinances.

Another aspect of the original and somewhat complicated rules that
had already been changed, was the category of 'middle grade' of
woman worker, termed by Dr Charteris the 'Woman Workers' Guild',
which was to have consisted of the most experienced workers in the
parish. This grade never really got off the ground. Instead, in 1907, kirk
sessions had been empowered to bestow on women of particular zeal,
ability and length of service (15 years minimum) a special Diploma and
badge—the Guild Leader's Diploma. By 1937 some 700 women had
received this coveted honour, and a Long Service Certificate, with
badge and bar, was instituted to reward 25 years of active work in the
Guild.

In 1920 Lady Polwarth retired as president, due to increasing deaf-
ness. She was succeeded by Miss Mary Lamond, a remarkable woman
who devoted her entire adult life to the Church and Guild and seemed
capable of doing any job that required filling. She became a deaconess in
1894, and succeeded Alice Maxwell as head of the Deaconess Training
House. She was honorary secretary of the Guild for six years, and took
over from Mrs Charteris the editorship of the *Life and Work* Guild
Supplement (which in 1926 was superseded by *Woman's Work in the
Church*). Mary Lamond started the tradition whereby the president did
the rounds of all the Presbyterial Councils during her term of office
—indeed, it was Mary Lamond who invented Presbyterial Councils in
the first place. Before her time, the Guild branches were loosely
grouped into large provincial councils which each sent a representative
to the Guild Central Committee in Edinburgh; but in 1924 Mary
Lamond divided the provincial councils into smaller councils based on
the Presbytery. The Central Committee now had representatives from
every part of Scotland, making it a genuine 'parliament' of the Guild,
and in 1925 Presbyterial Councils were formed. Mary Lamond's travels
round the Councils set the pace for the modern presidential marathon,
which was wryly described to me by one former national president as
'squeezing the last drop of blood out of every national president!'

By 1927 there were 53 Presbyterial Councils, 927 branches and 55 000
members of the Woman's Guild; 64 Sections affiliated with the
Mothers' Union; 218 branches of the Girls' Guild, with 6667 members
and 13 of their own Presbyterial Councils; and 132 branches of the
Junior Guild with 3390 members.

These were hard times. The country was in the depths of depression and social unrest following the General Strike of 1926. Unemployment was desperately high, and social welfare pitifully low. The kind hearts and busy fingers of Guildswomen throughout the country were constantly employed in helping to ease the misery of the poor and the sick. That year the Guild promised to supply the Deaconess Hospital with enough linen for the next three years. Eighty-two members sent 52½ pairs of sheets, 54 bath towels, 136 pillowslips and £61 in cash. A single Guild, Castle in Campbeltown, knitted 40 pairs of stockings in 1928 for the local Bootless Fund, gave 49 other articles of clothing to the local Children's Welfare, provided clothing for 111 families, bedjackets and several large boxes of silver paper for the Deaconess Hospital, garments for the orphanage at Musselburgh, £4 10*s* worth of goods for the Country Market, and groceries and clothing for a local deaconess.

Miss Lamond also decided that something had to be done about the continuing 'seelence' of many Guildswomen; too few of them were willing and able to speak in public. The 1928 Report underlined the lack, using the new interest in radio to emphasise the point: 'The Guild has grievously felt the want of human wireless sets with loud speakers attached to broadcast its messages'. A Sub-Committee on Service was formed, and four study schools arranged, to train Guild members in public speaking and voice production and to give them an opportunity of practising their new skills in group discussions. Miss Lamond's aim was to build up in every Council a nucleus of speakers who could be sent out to address the smaller meetings and thus save the president and her HQ staff for larger gatherings and tours.

The demands on the president, her four vice-presidents (representing the four main committees of the Guild) and Miss Bruce, the secretary at Guild headquarters in 22 Queen Street, Edinburgh, were constant and exacting—and particularly so at this historic time; because at long last the wheels were really moving towards the long-awaited union of the Church of Scotland and the United Free Church. As early as 1926, Miss Lamond and Miss Bruce had been meeting with the women's leaders of the UF Church to work out ways of joining forces when the time came. The UF had no single organisation of women like the Woman's Guild; instead, it ran a series of women's meetings in the congregations under various titles, represented on Presbyterial Committees and loosely grouped under a Women's Joint Committee. For months on end this committee and Miss Lamond's committee discussed and deliberated and prayed over how best to merge the two systems so that everyone would be happy. As the date for union—2 October 1929—came closer, women speakers from both Churches went all over the country in pairs, explaining the new set-up to their members.

What it boiled down to was that the Woman's Guild would be carried on in the new united Church of Scotland, based as before on the Branch in the congregation and the Council in the Presbytery. Every Council would have four committees (Foreign Mission, Jewish Mission, Home Mission and Temperance) acting under the respective women's committees of the General Assembly.

At the time of the union the Guild had four national vice-presidents; so four UF ladies were appointed vice-presidents, too, to make things even. But eight were found to be far too many for practical purposes, and the number was gradually reduced to two, by retirement and what would now be called 'natural wastage'.

The historic moment of union between the two Churches was celebrated at a special Assembly on 2 October 1929, on neutral ground —a huge hall in Annandale Street in Edinburgh. The Lord High Commissioner was the Duke of York (later King George VI), and the Moderator was Dr John White, minister of the Barony Glasgow; along with Principal Alexander Martin of the United Free Church, he had been the chief architect of the union.

Mary Lamond was the only woman to speak at this momentous occasion. According to the official record: 'Miss Lamond brilliantly vindicated women's place in the Church by a speech of very singular power and charm'.

The act of Union that day brought more than half a million new members into the Church of Scotland, making a total of 1 300 000 —more than a third of the adult population of Scotland at that time. With 'adherents' (non-communicants) and children added, the Church of Scotland could claim the allegiance of nearly half the nation.[3] The union had its disruptive effects as well, however; there were inevitable upheavals as two churches became one, as some churches had to close, as new churches had to be built. Every congregation did not take kindly to amalgamation. Old loyalties and habits died hard, and it took more than a generation for many people to readjust.

The same problems faced the Woman's Guild. Some UF women refused to join the Guild; others joined, but continued to hold their own women's meetings (which exist to this day), often as afternoon gatherings for older women. In some cases, although a Guild was started in a merged congregation, the two groups of women never really gelled as a unit—until the next war, when differences were forgotten and a new camaraderie was forged in the common cause of running canteens and making comforts for the troops. But in general the re-union worked remarkably well and gave the Guild a tremendous boost, both in the size of its membership and in the influx of many women of abundant enthusiasm, vitality and new ideas. In 1930, 298 new branches of the Guild were formed, bringing the total to 1474 with a membership of 85 047; by the time of the Guild jubilee in 1937, the membership had risen to 127 557.

Having seen the union ship safely into harbour, Mary Lamond retired in 1932, after instituting another great Guild tradition—the mass meeting of Guildswomen during Assembly week. From 1891, the year of the first conference, Guild conferences had been held every second year (but occasionally annually) and at various times of the year, in all the cities and large towns in Scotland, as well as in London in 1903. There was always a Guild reception in Edinburgh during Assembly week, attended mainly by branch presidents and council representatives who tended to be ministers' wives accompanying their Assembly-bound husbands. The vast increase in Guild membership after the union made the usual conferences inadequate, however; so Mary Lamond decided on a Guild gathering during the 1932 Assembly that would accommodate more Guildswomen than had ever before been gathered together under one roof. With great daring the Central Committee booked the Usher Hall, and a new tradition was born. The Lord High Commissioner to the General Assembly, and the Moderator (that year he was the Guild's own missionary, Dr Graham of Kalimpong), went to the Usher Hall in all their panoply to visit the ladies and shower them with greetings, praise and jolly Moderatorial jokes. It was a huge success. From then on it became the official annual conference, and attendances increased every year until it became the all-ticket, four day affair it is today. In 1935 when the Duke of Kent (later to die in a war-time air crash) was Lord High Commissioner, there were 3500 Guildswomen in the Usher Hall, with an overflow meeting and part of the programme being broadcast by the BBC.

There was one disappointment, however, that marred the end of Mary Lamond's distinguished presidency and irked Guildswomen for many a day thereafter: a petition for Guild representatives and other women members of committees to be invited to sit in the General Assembly as corresponding members was turned down by that same 1932 Assembly. It would be more than 50 years before this right would be granted.

On her retirement, Miss Mary Lamond was made honorary president of the Guild, and settled down to study Hebrew—so that she could read the Psalms in the original. She also read them in French. And, as one of her sister deaconesses recalled after Miss Lamond's death in 1948, 'a favourite book when sleep was denied was *The Decline and Fall of the Roman Empire*'.

Miss Mary Lamond was only the first of a varied gallery of national leaders to rise to the top of the Charteris pyramid. The next to head the biggest organisation of women in the land was a ploughman's daughter.

Notes to Chapter 11

1 Reproduced by kind permission of Miss Harvey's sister, Mrs Marjory James
2 Mrs Horatio Macrae, *Alice Maxwell, Deaconess* (Hodder & Stoughton, 1919), p. 186
3 J M Reid, *Kirk & Nation* (Skeffington, 1960), p. 167

12

New Blood

Mrs L B Meredith was born Lizzie Buist Graham in 1884, the eldest of the six children of a ploughman at Milton of Aberdalgie, in Perthshire (her father later became a gasworks manager in Fife). From the local primary school, Lizzie Graham went on to Sharp's Institution in Perth, where the headmaster wrote of her: 'I have seldom had a more zealous, painstaking and deserving pupil'. Her calling was to be a teacher; so, as a child of the United Free Church, she went to do her teacher-training at the UF Church Training College at Moray House in Edinburgh. Her record there was mind-boggling: never absent, never late, 'first student and premier prizewoman in each year of her course'. At the end of her course she emerged qualified to teach French and German, arithmetic, algebra and geometry, advanced chemistry, geography, piano, Swedish drill, handwork, English, phonetics, history, practical physics, botany, zoology, needlework, Bible and catechism, cookery and singing! She taught at the Burgh Academy, Kilsyth, and at Moffat Academy, and managed to fit in degree courses at the University of St Andrews in English, French, German, education and moral philosophy.

Festooned with college accolades like 'exemplary, excellent, singular force and impressiveness', what a prize she would have made for the United Free Church! Instead she married a Church of Scotland minister, the Revd Thomas Meredith, and was soon employing her formidable talents in running branches of the Woman's Guild wherever her husband ministered—Dundee, Lochee, Inchture, and St Luke's, Comely Bank, in Edinburgh. She eventually climbed the Guild pyramid to become senior vice-president to Miss Lamond during the long period of negotiations with the UF Church towards union; and after she succeeded Miss Mary Lamond in 1932, the vast strides made by the Guild during the seven years of her presidency (1932–39) were due in no small measure to the calibre of women from Lizzie Meredith's former Church who duly came swinging in to swell the ranks.

One such woman was Mrs Davie Macleod, an Edinburgh woman with a totally different social background to that of the ploughman's daughter from Perthshire. 'Davie' (a family pet name, and the only one she ever used) was born a Lorimer, daughter of an Edinburgh advocate who became Sheriff-Principal of Aberdeen and Banff. Her cousin was the eminent Greek scholar, Professor William Lorimer, who translated the New Testament into Scots. The family lived in a fine house in Gloucester Place, in Edinburgh's New Town, with a nanny and servants. The girls went to the very modern St George's School for Girls, where Davie Lorimer was captain of hockey and one of a new breed of upper-class school-educated Scots girls, highly articulate, free-thinking and independent. The Lorimers were Liberals and United Free Kirkers, members of Free St George's; Mrs Lorimer was president of the Women's Foreign Mission, her daughters were members of the lively UF Girls' Auxiliary, which was founded by Davie's sister Eleanor and her friend Bessie Hogg. Inspired by the World Mission Conference of 1910 (forerunner of the World Council of Churches), Davie went off in 1915 to be a UF missionary teacher in India, and returned when she was in her forties to address the 1929 General Assembly of the UF Church; and then, to everyone's surprise (and her own, too, perhaps) she married a Highland minister in the newly united Church of Scotland. He was a widower with four children.

As the wife of the Revd Donald Macleod, Davie started the Woman's Guild at Applecross in Wester Ross, one of the most inaccessible parishes in Scotland; and in the years of expansion that followed the Union she helped to start many others in the Highlands. Sailing across stormy waters, or driving her old family Morris in all weathers over high mountain passes and impossible roads, she introduced women in remote parishes to Guild ideas and ideals, skills and interests. She taught them how to speak in public, how to run a committee; she encouraged girls to go on to higher education, or to go in for nursing instead of becoming domestic servants. Nothing would stop her attending the launch of a new Guild she had gently bullied into being. For instance, in the winter of 1933 she drove across the hills from Applecross to hansel a new Guild at Loch Carron; next morning the weather was so bad that the road home was blocked. Nothing daunted, she took the train to Kyle of Lochalsh to catch the boat to Stornoway which could drop her off at Applecross en route. But now the storm was so severe that the ferry from Applecross could not come out to meet the steamer; so it was on to Stornoway, pitching and tossing in the mountainous seas, then back to Kyle of Lochalsh after a second failed attempt to land at

Applecross. It was only on the next trip that she managed to get home to Applecross.

She was an excellent public speaker, and gave a memorable address in the Usher Hall on her perennial theme: that women must fulfil their potential, that they must never waste their talents. She herself was always learning something new. She had never done any housework or even cooked a meal before her marriage; so, at the age of 46, she took a bride's course at Atholl Crescent in Edinburgh before taking over the manse at Applecross. When she went into hospital in Skye at the age of 94, she said: 'I've decided today not to learn anything new'. She died two weeks later, after reciting the whole of A E Housman's poem, 'Loveliest of trees, the cherry now', to her step-daughter Mona—who had married Dr Roderick Smith, the minister of Loch Carron and later minister emeritus of Braid Church, Edinburgh.

Another of the great band of willing workers from the United Free Church was Miss Chris Lawson, who personified the Church of Scotland's genius for recruiting paid staff who were devoted to the Church and dedicated to the cause and prepared to work for it in all their leisure time as well as during their modestly-paid working hours. Chris Lawson came from service in the Home Mission of the UF Church to be secretary of the Women's Home Mission of the Church of Scotland from 1929 until her death in 1947. Throughout these years, according to her sister Nan, 'she devoted her life to her work and addressing Guild meetings all over Scotland. I think it would be impossible to find anyone who spoke to more Woman's Guilds than Chris did'.

What she spoke about was her work for the Home Mission, in which she had full charge of organising the conditions of service and the training of Church Sisters, missions to fisher girls and berry-pickers, social centres for factory girls, hostels for construction workers in Orkney and transit workers in Glasgow, forestry workers in Brechin and ATS girls invalided out of the army during the Second World War. She told the Guildswomen about the nurseries and toddlers' playgrounds she had organised, and enlisted their support for every new project embarked upon by her committee. It was no exaggeration when the Very Revd Dr John White described her death as 'an irreparable loss'; a chapel was built in her memory at the Deaconess Rest House in Greenhill Gardens in Edinburgh.

It was with doughty workers like these that Mrs Lizzie Meredith led her growing army of women towards the Guild Jubilee celebrations in 1937. Even the Usher Hall was too small for the mass meeting that year. It was held instead in the Waverley Market, and was attended by 7000 women, who proudly handed over cheques for £7000 which they had collected—half to build a two-bed ward in the Deaconess Hospital (first claim on beds for Guild members, second for foreign missionaries), and the other half for Kalimpong.

Lizzie Meredith also endeared herself to Guildswomen by her forth-right efforts to free them from subservience to the Christian Life and Work Committee, whose convener (a man, of course) even chaired meetings of the Central Committee, the Guild's own 'parliament'. Lizzie Meredith failed to persuade the General Assembly that it was high time the Guild reported directly to the Assembly instead of through the Life and Work Committee; but in 1935 the Assembly made one concession, at least, and she became the first Guild president to chair her own Central Committee. She gained another advance in 1939 when the Guild was given responsibility for its own management and finances. Each branch, on registration, was to contribute towards the general expenses of the Woman's Guild a sum of five shillings if the membership was under 25, and ten shillings if it was over 25. Branch contributions were increased over the years, becoming a capitation fee which was doubled in 1986 to one pound per member. These contributions are the Guild's only source of income for financing its office administration and paying the salaries of its office staff, which in the centenary year consists of an organising secretary, an assistant secretary, a part-time cashier, two part-time office assistants—and a word-processor.

Another change that was made in the Constitution in 1939 placed a limit of four years on any individual presidency. Lizzie Meredith was the last president to serve for more than four years.

The new Constitution also recognised the Guild Secretary as a member of the Central Committee and of all sub-committees, with full voting powers—thus recognising, at long last, the special and in-dispensable part played by successive national secretaries ever since the Guild's inception.

The very first secretary had been a man, George McAlpine (1887 –92), who was appointed by Dr Charteris from the Christian Life and Work Committee office. The first woman secretary was Miss Ethel McInroy (1892–96), who helped Mrs Charteris through the hectic early years of organisation as well as being secretary of the Kalimpong Mission, responsible for gathering in all the contributions of goods and cash and their transport to India; she kept on this job after retiring as Guild secretary, continued speaking to the branches, became president of the Angus and Mearns Guild Council—and died as a result of a bicycle accident in 1926. Her successor, Miss Margaret Johnston (1896–1906), had made a great impression on Guildswomen at a conference in Kirkcaldy in 1894 with a stirring speech on 'The Duties of the Guildswoman as Daughter'. She retired in 1906 to take charge of the inebriate women at the Guild Cottage, became a deaconess, and travelled to the Middle East, Africa and India, visiting mission stations. She was succeeded by the redoubtable Miss Mary Lamond (1906–12), who was followed in her turn by another deaconess, Miss Jane Dods (1912–20), who saw the Guild through the upheavals of the First World War.

Miss Cunningham, who was secretary from 1920 until her marriage in 1925, had to organise the first Presbyterial Councils. Miss J M Bruce (1925–34) had all the union negotiations to deal with. Miss Martin (1934–45) masterminded the mammoth Guild Jubilee celebrations in 1937 as well as seeing the Guild through the Second World War; and the next secretary, Mrs Janet Sim, simply masterminded everything! Mrs Sim served for 20 years, from 1945 to 1965. She was a minister's wife, a long-standing member of the Guild and formidably knowledgeable about its affairs. She was an obvious candidate for national president, but when her husband died she had no choice but to take on paid employment as secretary. And what a secretary she was! She was guide, friend, manager, a mine of information and mentor to six national presidents and thousands of Guildswomen. Her length of service to the Guild was exceeded only by an assistant secretary, Marjorie Gardner, who served at 22 Queen Street and then 121 George Street for 37 years (1926–63).

The secretaries who followed the remarkable Mrs Sim—Mrs 'Bunty' Inglis (1965–74), Mrs Joyce Town (1974–76) and Mrs Kathleen Beveridge (1976–85)—were all in the long tradition of indefatigable, all-purpose Guild organisers: managing, Minute-taking, scurrying from meeting to meeting, and always finding the time to be helpful to visiting Guildswomen, researchers and old ladies who just wanted a look at 'yon lot at 121'. The most recent secretary of the first hundred years, Mrs Lorna Paterson, a Guild member and wife of the minister of St Michael's, Linlithgow, took up the job in 1985 just in time to have to organise the Guild's centenary celebrations.

Mrs Lizzie Meredith retired as president in 1939. She was appointed honorary president of the Guild in 1955, and died in Perth in 1977, in the Guild's 90th birthday year, at the age of 94. A special fund was instituted in her memory, and was used to help finance Guild training sessions at Carberry House in the 1970s and '80s.

Mrs Meredith's successor was the youngest president in the Guild's history: Miss Allison Lyon Harvey, who was only 37 years old when she took over the leadership of 140 000 Guildswomen in 2000 branches.

She was the elder daughter of Captain Thomas Harvey, of Polmont, the convener of Stirling County Council, and was a great-grand-daughter of a former Moderator of the Free Church and a grand-daughter of a former Rector of the Edinburgh Academy. She was tall, slim and attractive, with unusually beautiful eyes, and had a pleasant voice that could carry clearly to the back of a hall without a micro-phone. She had learned her speaking skills early, for she was one of the leaders of the bright, intelligent breed of young church girls who built up the Girls' Guild after the First World War. She was its president from 1926–28 (and automatically a member of the Woman's Guild Central Committee), and when the Girls' Guild united with the UF Girls' Auxiliary she was made president of the new Girls' Association, from 1930–32. She was a missionary for three years in India and served at Kalimpong (where she survived a crash-landing in the jungle); when she returned to Scotland in 1939, she joined the Woman's Guild and was promptly offered the presidency: 'I think they were only too glad to find someone with enough time to devote to the work,' she modestly explained to a newspaper reporter.

But the elders of the Guild knew well what they were doing when they chose this quick-minded, strong and resourceful young woman, and they were blessing their choice a few months later when the Second World War broke out: women were called up, church halls comman-deered, evening meetings abandoned because of the blackout and air-raids. But Allison Harvey battled on, undaunted, dealing with the correspondence at 121 George Street, chairing committee meetings, travelling here, there and everywhere round the branches in her old Ford Prefect (its number plate was WG1); and when her petrol ration ran out she spent hours in unheated, blacked-out trains, often shunted into sidings on lonely, snowbound routes. With the family home (Weedingshall, in Polmont) commandeered by the RAF, Allison Har-vey made her headquarters with friends in Airth, in Stirlingshire. During the summer of 1940 the Guild raised £3800 for Church of Scotland huts and canteens: two for men and one for women serving in Orkney, and two mobile canteens, one in Scotland and one in the Middle East. Allison Harvey was in charge of the mobile canteen based in Stirlingshire, and travelled with it to help the victims of the blitz on Glasgow, Clydebank and Greenock.

As always in times of national emergency, Guildswomen were busy knitting and sewing furiously. The Board of Trade authorised the Woman's Guild to issue vouchers allowing members to buy wool to knit for the troops without having to give up their meagre clothing coupons. Over 80 000 vouchers were issued. In addition to all this khaki and blue knitting, Shetland Guildswomen were still sending beautiful Shetland woollens to be sold in aid of Guild schemes, as they had been doing since the Guild began. In 1943 the Shetland Sub-Committee, which had been formed to market the Shetland goods, sold a record £778-worth, and most of the money went to the Maintenance of the Ministry Fund.

There was no Annual Meeting between 1939 and 1943, but area meetings were held in Musselburgh, Inverness, Dumfries, Hamilton, Perth, Aberdeen, Dunoon, Glasgow, Kilmarnock and Galashiels, and despite blackout, air-raids and poor transport, they were well attended. Committees continued to meet, and a remarkable amount of business was carried on through the darkest days.

Allison Harvey completed her term of office in 1943, and went off to finish the war as a chaplain's assistant in the ATS, serving at home and in Germany. She came home to be president of the Women's Foreign Mission, and a vice-convener of the Foreign Mission Committee; she was deeply involved in the ecumenical movement, and represented the Kirk at several world conferences. She was a founder-member of the Scottish Churches House at Dunblane. At her funeral in Dunblane Cathedral in 1974, the Very Revd Dr John Gray said of Allison Harvey: 'Had she turned her great gifts to her own advancement she could have had a successful career in politics or industry. But she had been brought up to serve the Church and the community, and right well she did so'.

The successor to Allison Harvey's presidency of the Guild was Mrs Elizabeth McKerrow. She was a founder-member of the Woman's Guild of Wellington Church in Glasgow, a huge branch with nearly 600 members. As national president, Mrs McKerrow inherited a Guild reduced in membership by about 30 000 since the start of the war, but with an increasing number of branches and a feeling in the air of great things to come as soon as the women and girls came back from the war. The Guild was keenly interested in the Beveridge Report with its blueprint for the Welfare State, and there were deep discussions on the effect it might have on the Guild's social work. When Ernest Bevin, the Minister of Labour, called a conference of 6000 women in the Albert Hall in London in 1943 to announce his post-war reconstruction plans, he included 90 members of the Woman's Guild—the first Government recognition, since early Temperance days, of the Guild's importance in the field of social service. A joint committee of Woman's Guild and Youth was set up in 1945 to help women build up a 'happy Christian home life', and the Guild gave £5762 to church extension, and £3433 to Christian Reconstruction in Europe, while the Shetland knitters broke all records with sales of £1185.

With the end of the war in Europe in 1945, membership of the Guild began to increase. A conference to help Guildswomen with their public speaking was held in 1946, and a training school for younger Guildswomen in 1947. That year—her last as president—Elizabeth McKerrow represented the Guild at the Annual Conference of the National Council of Women, and the Guild helped provide material requested by the World Council of Churches for a book on the life and work of women in the Church.

The country was still in the post-war doldrums, with food rationing, utility clothes, utility furniture and power-cuts, but Guild spirits were lifted by a wonderful Thanksgiving service in 1947 to celebrate the 60th anniversary of the Guild. It was held in the West Kirk, Greenock, the presbytery of the new national president, Mrs Anne Sutherland (later Mrs Jacobs, when she was widowed and married an ex-Provost of Greenock), and it was broadcast by the BBC. This service had a tremendous rallying effect on women listening in their homes, and next year the Guild's membership went up by over 9000. In the following year it rose by another 8000. Women queued to get into the Annual Meeting in the Usher Hall, and an overflow meeting had to be held for the hundreds who failed to get in.

Hand in hand with the post-war restrictions came the growth of bureaucracy. The Board of Trade was making difficulties for the sale of Shetland goods at a time of clothes rationing, and the Shetland depot at 121 George Street had to be closed down; but the Guild was now busy sewing for refugee children in Europe. Twenty-two sacks of children's clothing were despatched in 1948, and after three German church-women had visited Scotland, describing post-war conditions in their own defeated cities, the Guild sent 3000 layettes and 50 sacks of clothing to German mothers as an act of reconciliation.

As the church extensions scheme strove to provide for the movement of people to large new housing estates, churches in older districts had to close down or unite with other churches, causing a reduction in the number of Guild branches; but the membership total was still increasing, and the first Guild branch to be formed in a hospital was opened in 1949 in the Southern General in Glasgow. Two more hospital Guilds were started in 1950: in Wedderburn House, Musselburgh, and Crookston Cottage Homes, Glasgow. A brand-new Guild magazine, dedicated to recording news of the branches, appeared in 1950, called the *Guild Bulletin*. And in 1951 there was a brand-new national president: Mrs Lois Jarvis.

13

Time to Breathe

In 1951, the year in which she became national president, Mrs Lois Jarvis talked about herself in a radio broadcast on the old BBC Scottish Home Service, in a series entitled *Why I Believe*[1]:

> I am no theologian; I am no trained thinker: I am an ordinary simple woman. . . . There are a great many things in the world I do not understand: physics and chemistry are mysteries to me; I am absolutely hopeless at mathematics; machinery and electricity are miracles to me!
>
> There are, of course, a great many things in the Bible and in the Christian creed that I don't understand. But I know at least that the Christian values and way of life are the best that I have heard about, or seen. I can't argue about them very well with clever people—all the same, that is what I believe. It often seems to me that people make too much of their intellectual difficulties. Intellect isn't everything!
>
> My creed is a very simple one. I believe in God through Jesus Christ. That satisfies me. I do not remember the time when I did not know about Jesus, when I was not encouraged to look to Him as my example and to speak to him as my Friend. . . . It isn't so much that I hold Christian beliefs, as that I am held by them.

She went on to say that the eldest of her four sons had been killed in the war in Italy; and she told her listeners how she had *known* of his death, three days before the dreaded telegram arrived:

> One afternoon, sitting by the fire talking to friends, I suddenly heard him calling to me. I looked up at his photograph. I knew something had happened to him. . . . Yet people do not believe in the spiritual side of life. I wonder why? If a son's spirit can call to a mother from a distant country, surely it is not so strange that there is One unseen, whose Spirit is calling to us!

Her simple faith struck a chord in thousands of listening mothers, and endeared her to her huge family of Guildswomen. They knew she was neither as simple nor as ordinary as she made out. She was a daughter of the manse, wife of Dr Ernest Jarvis, the much-loved minister of Wellington Church in Glasgow (which had already given the Guild a national president in the person of Elizabeth McKerrow). She was well-educated (at St Leonard's in St Andrews), she had been trained in the Froebel method of primary school teaching, she was an extremely talented artist and a very good public speaker. She was also a warm-hearted, motherly, gracious lady who identified naturally and effortlessly with the simple, ordinary women who formed the bulk of the Guild. She understood them, and she knew that what they wanted after the years of war and shortages and austerity was, above all, space to breathe again, time to lick wounds and heal broken hearts, a return to safe, familiar surroundings and simple, familiar pleasures.

For them, the Guild represented comfortable continuity and security. Its membership was at a record post-war peak of 150 000. It was an institution now, firmly settled into the fabric of the Church, second only to the kirk session in importance in the parish, with its own set of traditions and procedures and ways of doing things. It was not exactly a closed society, but like all long-established institutions it had a mystique and an aura of exclusiveness about it which could frighten off outsiders—and which unnerved many a minister's young wife who found herself president of the local Guild, willy-nilly, in her earliest days as a manse bride.

Change was on the way, of course. The swinging '60s and the permissive '70s were just around the corner. Why, even in the '50s, some ministers' wives were refusing to become automatic presidents of the local Guild, or even refusing to join the Woman's Guild altogether!

But that was for the new generation who were beginning to rise to the top of the pyramid. Under Lois Jarvis, the Guild had four years of happy consolidation and growing membership. Each year the Usher Hall was bursting at the seams. Using her talents as a teacher and communicator, Mrs Jarvis entranced her members with gaily illustrated leaflets which she designed herself; the one which she wrote to show delegates and members how the Guild worked, entitled *The Tale of Daisie and Maisie*, is treasured in the Guild's archives as a classic of its kind. She also wrote little plays and pageants about the Guild, with the members dressing up as fisher girls and deaconesses; her dramatic presentation, *What is the Woman's Guild?*, brought the house down at the Annual Meeting of 1953 and started a new tradition of leavening the diet of speeches with a little entertainment.

These were heady days. Lois Jarvis was in Westminster Abbey for the Coronation in 1953 and 100 Guildswomen had places on the royal route; and when the Queen made her Coronation visit to Scotland that year, the Guild was well represented in the historic service in the High Kirk of St Giles. In 1954, Lois Jarvis was interviewed about the Woman's Guild on the brand-new Scottish Television channel.

By a quirk of history, Lois Jarvis effectively missed out on the last year of her presidency. Her husband, Dr Ernest Jarvis, was appointed Moderator of the General Assembly of the Church of Scotland, and Mrs Jarvis realised that she would be unable to accompany her husband on his Moderatorial rounds and fulfil all her presidential duties. So she chose a deputy, her close friend Mrs Ailsa Miller, wife of the minister of St Nicholas Church, Aberdeen; and it fell to Mrs Miller to welcome to the Annual Meeting not only the Moderator of the General Assembly but the National President of the Woman's Guild!

The end of Ailsa Miller's stand-in presidency was also the end of Lois Jarvis's term of office. The new president, Mrs Jessie Dingwall, was also a minister's wife. Thirty-one years after she became president, Jessie Dingwall was the star of the 1986 Annual Meeting, when she had the Guildswomen rolling in the aisles at her reminiscences of 60 years in the Guild. She told them of going to Shetland as a young bride and finding herself straightaway president of her first Guild. Still in her early twenties, and looking if anything ten years younger, she did not impress the Shetlanders much at first: the branch secretary, making her list of delegates to the Presbyterial Council, told her, 'We'll no' be pitten your name doon yet. Ah doot ye've a lot tae learn'.

'And so I had,' recalled Jessie Dingwall. 'I had a BSc degree, but what good is that for running a Guild?'

She recalled the time she washed a Moderator's lace cuffs when he visited Shetland just after attending upon the king at Balmoral. Mrs Dingwall asked him whether the brown stain on his cuff was tea or coffee. 'Neither,' he said proudly, 'that's Balmoral gravy.'

After Shetland, Jessie Dingwall moved to Dunblane and then to Glasgow, when her husband was appointed secretary of the Scottish Sunday School Union. They joined Wellington Church, and Mrs Dingwall became an enthusiastic member of Wellington Guild and a neighbour of the national president, Mrs Lois Jarvis. One day Mrs Jarvis told her over the garden wall: 'You're to follow me as national president—and I won't take No for an answer'. So the Guild got its third Wellington president.

Mrs Dingwall and her senior vice-president, Mrs Grace Hay, read the lessons at the historic dedication of the Woman's Guild Church in the vast Glasgow housing estate of Barlanark, in 1956. This new church was part of the Kirk's church extension scheme, and it was also the

Guild's memorial to Dr John White, whose idea it had been for the Guild to build a church of its own. It was a milestone occasion in the Guild's history—but Jessie Dingwall and Grace Hay almost missed it, because someone accidentally locked them inside the new vestry, and their desperate pounding on the door was only just heard in time to let them make a breathless entrance in the solemn procession led by the Very Revd Professor J Pitt-Watson. The Guild had raised £21 000 to build the church, which had a stained glass rose window symbolising women's service in the Church down the ages. The pulpit light was the gift of the Guild branch in Glasgow's Southern General Hospital.

Thirty years later, as the oldest living former president, Mrs Dingwall stood on the platform in the Assembly Hall. She was a tall, straight figure 'in her eighties' (that was as near as she would come to confessing her age), wearing an elegant dress and stylish picture hat, as Guildswomen had done at Annual Meetings in the 1950s, facing the hatless and gloveless delegates of the 1980s. For many onlookers, it epitomised in one vivid little cameo the tremendous change that had overtaken the Guild in the years between—not only a change of style and image, but a change of emphasis and direction, too,

Mrs Jessie Dingwall told the 1986 delegates that during her own term as president, the Guild had reached its highest-ever membership: a total of 160 000. That had been in 1956. The exact figure was 160 161—but it proved to be a short-lived peak. Within a year, membership had dropped to 153 180, and would continue to decline. Old churches were closing, and old branches were closing at the rate of 20 a year—and the new branches could not keep up with the pace of decline.

With historical hindsight, it is now possible to see the year 1956 as a watershed in the affairs of the Guild. Nothing would ever be the same again.

In the following year, the Guild helped Glasgow Social Service Committee to build a new maternity unit for unmarried mothers in Landsdown House, and Mrs Dingwall performed the opening ceremony. But the new welfare state was taking over; much of the caring pioneered by Guildswomen was becoming the province of professional social workers, or about to be gathered into the vast empire of the Church of Scotland's department of Social Responsibility. The countries of the foreign missions were gaining their independence one by one, and that field of service, too, became part of one huge Kirk operation under its Overseas Council (later the Board of World Mission and Unity). Missionary doctors and teachers would soon be going out to India and Africa only at the invitation of the Churches of these countries, and the day was not far distant when African and Indian and

West Indian missionaries would start coming to Scotland to preach Christianity at the invitation of the Kirk. The leaders of the Woman's Guild would soon be questioning its whole reason for being.

Also in 1957, the General Assembly sent an 'overture anent women and the eldership' down to the Presbyteries for discussion, and the Guild circulated a leaflet around the branches, setting out the arguments for and against women becoming elders. The argument went on for another four years before Assembly approval was finally given in 1961; and one of the first women to be ordained an elder in Wellington Church, Glasgow, was Mrs Jessie Dingwall.

Note to Chapter 13

1 *Why I Believe: A Symposium of Christian Belief* (Epworth Press, 1952), pp 33-38

14

Age and Image

When Mrs Dingwall retired from the presidency in 1959, to be succeeded by Mrs Grace Hay, the membership of the Guild had dropped back to 150 000. But a new item appeared in the Guild Annual Report for that year: 'Mothers' Groups—7066 members'. Mothers' Groups had been sprouting in churches ever since the end of the war; and the Woman's Guild, mindful of its failure in the early years to develop a mothers' union that truly belonged to the Guild, was determined to make the Young Mothers' Fellowships, as they came to be called, an integral part of the Guild.

The main problem was one of age. What exactly was a 'young mother'? Did the 'young' refer to the age of the mother, or to the age of the children? And at what age should a Young Mother become a fully-fledged Guildswoman? At first the Central Committee ruled, in 1959, that a mother was expected to leave the Fellowship for the Guild when her youngest child reached the age of eight. This caused such dissatisfaction that eventually, in 1972, the age of the children was dropped as a criterion, and members were allowed to stay in the fellowship for ten years, or until they were '35 to 40' years old. But even this tactful expedient of letting women leave without having to declare their exact age failed to please everyone. Middle-aged mothers felt that 'going up' to the Guild would label them as 'elderly'; so they simply refused to go, and stayed on, and on, as not-so-young mothers. When Guild headquarters tried to apply pressure about the age limit, some Young Mothers' groups simply disbanded, or disaffiliated from the Guild and continued on their own.

Those Fellowships which toed the line and worked within the rules set down by the Guild went from strength to strength, and the keenest of their leaders moved up the pyramid to occupy important positions in the Woman's Guild. Numbers expanded, too: in 1959 there were 267 Fellowships in operation. In 1962 they were given their own Constitution, binding them as part of the Woman's Guild, and declaring as their aim: 'To encourage Christian home and family life and to unite its members, through worship, fellowship and service'.

The Constitution also gave them their first representation on the Guild's Central Committee. One Young Mother was to serve as a co-opted member for two years. The first one appointed was Mrs May Smith, of St Philip's Mothers' Fellowship at Joppa, Edinburgh (who was to rise to become national president of the Guild in 1984). Representation on the Central Committee was increased in 1968 to 10, and in 1970 to 20 Young Mothers. By this time the Constitution had been revised to allow the inclusion of young childless wives in 1965, and the Young Mothers became the Young Wives and Mothers Group. The rules were changed again in 1972 to include all women, married or unmarried, under the '35–40' age limit, and the name became the Young Woman's Group. From that time onwards the Guild would be referred to as 'The Branch' and the Young Women as 'The Group'.

In that year, 1972, the Young Women reached a peak of 905 Groups with 27 150 members, but after that it started to decline, in line with the falling membership of the Guild itself. As well as the general decline in church membership and church attendance, the Guild was suffering from a very real Age Gap—a yawning abyss that stopped middle-aged women from joining the Branch and kept them hanging on in the Groups, where their very presence made the Groups seem more elderly and less attractive for younger women to join. It was a classic vicious circle.

The trouble with any organisation that lasts for a hundred years is that people tend to confuse its age with its attitudes. The 'elderly' tag has increasingly come to be attached to the Guild as it has advanced in years. Yet when Dr Charteris started the Guild, one of the reasons for its slow development was exactly the opposite complaint: because it was a young organisation, people thought that it must be meant only for young women! An item in the *Guild Supplement* of 1896 desperately tried to put the record straight:

> We have in our ranks a member over ninety years of age, who walked four or five miles to bring two pairs of baby socks she had knitted for the Work Party. Surely Lily Cooper is the senior worker of the Church! Surely, we may add, no one will now think the Guild is only for young women!

Ironically, it is thanks to a century of Lily Coopers that no one has thought of the Guild for many a long year as a place for young women. Every branch has its modicum of elderly members: loyal, long-serving, never-absent, no longer able to take an active part in things but mindful of old glories and sticklers for cherished traditions, who would no more think of leaving the Guild, or missing their 'Guild night', than failing to keep up their life insurance payments. Some of the oldest members are loved and cherished and honoured by their fellow-Guildswomen, like 93-year-old Mrs Jane Taylor of St Nicholas, Aberdeen, who 'has a sore leg every other day, but never on Guild Tuesday'; Mrs Crichton, aged 93 and still attending Skene Branch, Aberdeenshire; Mrs Buchan, a 92-year-old 'regular' at Crimond, Fraserburgh, where the famous tune for Psalm 23 was composed; Mrs McCurdy, 92-year-old doyen of Kirkliston, West Lothian; Miss Mary Gibson, of Kilbarchan—'not quite a hundred years old, but quite old!'; Miss Murray, of Balmaclellan, Castle Douglas, who was still Branch secretary in 1984 when she was 88; Mrs Annie Purvis, enjoying her visits to the Guild at Cardenden, Fife, in her 99th year; Mrs James Yuill, of St James, Falkirk, clocking-in regularly at 92; Mrs Semple, at 90, still baking for Guild functions at Torrance, Stirlingshire; and Mrs Margaret Brown, honorary president of Wardlawhill, Rutherglen, a Guildswoman there for 79 years, and looking forward to her 104th birthday in the Guild's centenary year.

These old-timers, and so many others down the years, were the backbone and life-blood of the Guild. The fact that an upper age-limit to exclude them has never been imposed is a tribute to the Guild's compassion and decency; but there is no doubt that the presence of so many elderly members has discouraged many a modern middle-aged woman from joining. It has probably been the fault of poor public relations at Branch level that many congregations do not really know what goes on in the Guild, and fail to appreciate that although all ages are welcome, there is usually a nucleus of younger, forward-looking women running the show—and that these Guildswomen are more knowledgeable about the affairs of the modern church and the social concerns of the day than most kirk sessions and the vast majority of men and women in the pews.

Under the new national president, Mrs Grace Hay (1959–63), Guildswomen were being encouraged as never before to look outwards to service in the wider community. Grace Hay, daughter of the Revd J McCallum Robertson of Regent Place Church in Glasgow's Dennistoun, wife of the Revd William Hay of Erskine Church, Falkirk, and mother of the Revd W J R Hay of Buchanan Church, Drymen, was a graduate of the University of Glasgow, with double honours in Latin and English. She was the first editor of the Guild's first real magazine, the *Guild Bulletin*, and in it she continually recorded the variety of jobs being done by Guildswomen in the community: in 1959, Guildswomen were working in the WVS, serving tea to blood donors, helping at child welfare clinics, mental hospitals and Borstal institutions. A survey of 94 Guilds in a rural area revealed 340 Guildswomen working for the WVS, 320 in the Red Cross, 156 on Old People's Welfare Councils, 95 in Civil Defence, 42 in the RSSPCC, and others on Youth Panels, Child Welfare Committees, War Pensions Committees, National Savings Groups and in local government.

At the same time, the familiar old Guild names were disappearing. In 1963 the Temperance and Morals Committee—successor to the pioneering Women's Temperance Association—merged with the Social Service Committee of the Church of Scotland to form the Social and Moral Welfare Board. Next year the Women's Foreign Mission and the Women's Jewish Mission—the dear old WFM and WJM —became part of the new Overseas Council, incorporating all the work of the Church overseas; the Women's Home Mission—the WHM, through which Guildswomen had supported the work of deaconesses since before the turn of the century—was now part of the Home Board. These larger administrative Kirk units were later reorganised and renamed as Boards of Social Responsibility, World Mission and Unity, and Ministry and Mission. The Woman's Guild continued to be represented on women's committees attached to these Boards, and to bring the work and the needs of the various departments before their members through their delegates to the annual meetings in Edinburgh. Guildswomen were also appointed to vice-convenerships on the Boards. But real authority and decision-making was effectively in the hands of men. After the admission of women to the eldership in 1966, and the ordination in 1969 of the first woman minister (a retired deaconess, Catherine McConnachie, in Aberdeenshire), roads would begin to open up to a future when women might play an equal part with men in all the affairs of the Church, and the Guild was soon to bring forth a clutch of leaders dedicated to hastening this very process; but all that seemed a very long way off back in 1963, when the Guild felt the old, familiar ground slipping from under its feet, and decided that the time had come to consider its future very seriously.

The national president at this critical period in the Guild's history was Mrs Isabel Douglas, whose husband, the late Dr Hugh Douglas, was to be Moderator of the General Assembly in 1970. Isabel Douglas was a talented young woman from Coldstream in Berwickshire, national vice-president of the Girls' Association when she was 18, and a graduate of the University of St Andrews with a degree in Modern and Medieval History. She could have settled into a comfortable and lucrative job as secretary of the family engineering company, but she preferred to take a social science diploma and go off to Glasgow—'tae wash dirty bairns' at

Glasgow University Settlement, as a disgusted uncle put it. For five years she lived in a room-and-kitchen, organised dances and youth clubs in Bridgeton, became a club leader for the Revd George MacLeod in Govan and Iona, and organised 300 girls and 60 helpers in the Pierce Institute six days and nights a week, for a salary of £120 a year. She married George MacLeod's assistant, and took over her first Guild at his first charge, St John's Church, Leven, in Fife.

As national president (1963–66), Isabel Douglas applied herself to the task of achieving a new unity in the Guild and redefining its aims and purposes. A Policy Committee was set up and charged with examining 'the Name, the Aim and the Organisation of the Woman's Guild in the light of changing patterns within the Church and Society'. The branches were consulted by means of questionnaires. The first decision that was taken was to keep the name 'Woman's Guild'. The Guild aim was updated to 'unite the women of the Church in the dedication of their lives to Jesus Christ through worship, fellowship and service', and Isabel Douglas had her own tenure at the top shortened by a new rule limiting presidents to three years in office. The need to give the Guild a greater sense of involvement with the whole work of the Church was achieved by inviting the women serving as vice-conveners of the three big Kirk Boards to be national vice-presidents of the Guild, along with the three vice-presidents appointed by the Central Committee. The Guild now had six vice-presidents, probably one of the most hard-working groups in the whole organisation. A succession of devoted senior vice-presidents down the years worked at least as hard as, if not harder than, the presidents they supported, while enjoying little of the limelight.

Isabel Douglas formed her six vice-presidents into a kind of Think Tank called the President's Group, and introduced the concept of a 'Theme for the Year'—an idea she had picked up in Australia, which gave the Guild a unity of purpose by annually supplying every branch with the same theme around which to build its year's activities. A Theme Booklet was published every year outlining a programme for the session, and this has become every branch president's indispensable guide and friend. This one simple but brilliant idea probably did more to engender a feeling of unity among Guildswomen than anything since the introduction of the Guild badge.

The task of putting the new ideas into effective action fell to the next president, Mrs Kathleen Grieve (1966–69), who was described in the *Glasgow Herald* in 1966 by the late Allison Downie thus:

> In appearance almost the perfect image of a typical Woman's Guild member—entering early middle-age, plump of figure, serene and

smiling, exuding an air of reassuring capability, Mrs Grieve is also outspoken, decisive, and clear-thinking.

Outspoken she certainly was, and impatient of those who wanted to cling to the past: 'A lot of old fuddie-duddies frantically knitting woolly vests for African babies under the tropical sun' was the image people had of the Guild, she told Guildswomen in Aberdeen. Kathleen Grieve was an Aberdeenshire woman herself, daughter of the medical superintendent of Tor-na-Dee Sanitorium. She graduated in botany and zoology at Aberdeen University, and worked as a technical assistant with the BBC in Aberdeen before marrying the Revd G M Denny Grieve and running Guilds in Kelso, Helensburgh and Glasgow.

She did not spare her fellow Guildswomen, in a series of hard-hitting comments and admonitions:

> Too many people sit in booked seats at their Guilds, never looking around them, nor meeting new people.
>
> Too much time is spent sitting listening and drinking tea. The Guild *must* educate its members to shoulder their responsibilities.
>
> 'What does the Woman's Guild do, anyway?' I am often asked. 'It holds meetings and it raises money. Surely there must be other things for them to do?'
>
> I wonder if we are not too apt to believe that making tablet or running snowball-teas is all that the Church asks of us as individuals?

It was a period of intense self-analysis and self-criticism, as Guild leaders tried to ginger up the troops for new challenges. Kathleen Grieve's pithy comments were delivered as she went storming round her presidential circuit by car, always accompanied by her mother who insisted, 'If you're going to be killed, I'll be killed with you!'

During Kathleen Grieve's presidency the familiar initials 'W G' took on a new meaning—Working Groups. Working Groups were set up to organise the Annual Meeting, the Theme Booklet, schedules, Central Committee conferences, to prepare a new Constitution for the Young Mothers, establish the Christian Women's Consultative Committee for women of all denominations in Scotland, prepare a new Guild Handbook and a new membership card, and to start up a new magazine —*Spotlight*. A new image of the Guild was beginning to emerge: at the 1968 Annual Meeting, when the Theme was 'The World in their Hands', the *Glasgow Herald* reported:

> Music from a pop group, a hard-hitting speech by a bearded young science student, jokes from the Archbishop of Canterbury—heavens, could this *really* be the Guild meeting?

Yes, it could, and it was. The times they were a-changing.

15

All Change

Mrs Elizabeth Anderson (1969–72) is the one and only Englishwoman to have become national president of the Woman's Guild of the Church of Scotland. Born in Yorkshire, she came to Scotland in 1941 to take a degree in Philosophy and Political Economy at the University of St Andrews, then went to Glasgow to run a Youth Club for the Young Women's Christian Association (YWCA) in Bridgeton. It was a tough assignment for a 20 year old with a Yorkshire accent, trying to tame young tearaways in the blackout of Glasgow's East End in the middle of the war; but Elizabeth survived a brush with a razor gang, and acquired 'the broadest Glasgow accent you ever heard', before marrying her young man, the Revd Grant Anderson, in 1945 and taking charge of her first Guild branch at Laurieknowe Church, Dumfries, when she was 22 years old. By 1966 she was senior vice-president of the Guild, and in that capacity she went to Uppsala in Sweden for the 1968 meeting of the World Council of Churches.

The experience 'turned me inside out', as she put it. She was so moved by the testimony of Third World delegates describing the plight of the hungry in their lands that she came back and produced a moving report that affected the Central Committee very profoundly. It was the reports of delegates like Elizabeth Anderson that gave tremendous impetus to the Christian Aid movement in the 1970s. The Central Committee's response was to dig deep into its coffers and allocate a quarter of the Guild's capital reserve—£2000—to buy a threshing mill for Jalna in India.

The enthusiastic response from Guild members to the Jalna mill project made it clear that the women wanted, above all, a *specific* object to work for, something they could identify with, and something for which they could raise a specific sum of money on their own. So, in 1969 (Elizabeth Anderson's first year as president), after due consultation with the Assembly's Stewardship and Budget Committee, the

'Annual Project' was born: a special yearly cause chosen by the Guild, to which they would send money after they had made a massive annual commitment to the Kirk's Mission and Service Fund.

The Annual Project brought back to the Guild something of the heady old days of Kalimpong fund-raising:

1969: A fund to help churches provide parish playgroups, now a thriving part of Church life.

1970: Furnishing the Kirk's rehabilitation centre in Edinburgh, Simpson House.

1971: Building dormitories and classrooms for the Kambui School for Deaf Children in Kenya.

1972: Providing funds for the Dundee Women's International Centre, the YWCA's Leith Walk Neighbourhood Centre in Edinburgh, and the Immigrants Centre in Glasgow.

1973: The Cosmobile—a motor caravan for the Parish Education Officer.

1974: Two specially designed cottages for the disabled in the grounds of Eastwoodhill Eventide Home in Giffnock.

1975: A 'Lighted Place' for quiet and meditation in the Chaplaincy Centre at Heriot-Watt University in Edinburgh.

1976: Improved living quarters at the Girls' School in Kalimpong, and new classrooms for the school at Mahakalguri.

1977: £21 716 for workshop centres for recovering alcoholics.

1978: In the International Year of the Child, £29 229 for the children of the Church at home and overseas.

1979: £36 427 to buy two houses, one for a retired minister, and one for a minister's widow.

1980: £21 774 to buy equipment for the new video venture of the Church of Scotland—the first Church to recognise the potential of video and set up its own video production department.

1981: £54 734 to build an operating theatre in the Church of South India's Rainy Hospital in Madras.

1982: £61 000 to provide beds for 35 homeless men, washing facilities and a fire escape in the People's Palace Night Shelter in Edinburgh's Cowgate.

1983: A chapel and extra accommodation in the Kirk's training centre, St Ninian's, in Crieff, costing £48 151.

1984: A four-fold project for which the Guild raised £59 303:

(1) Refurbishing the bathrooms in the Kirk's home for mentally handicapped young people in Keith Lodge, Stonehaven.

(2) Buying a van for deaconess Tilly Wilson's ministry to the travelling folk of Scotland.

(3) Funding a bursary through the Board of World Mission and Unity.

(4) Paying for a member of the Guild, Mrs Eleanor Butters, wife of the minister of Turriff, to spend two months visiting Christian women in Kenya.

The last Annual Project of the Guild century was to raise enough money to build ten extra bedrooms at the Kirk's Carberry Training Centre.

Having launched the first Annual Project in 1969, Elizabeth Anderson found herself becoming a pioneer in something which was to widen the whole field of Guild interest and take the movement into the new world of the politics of protest: women's rights, women's liberation, sexual equality, racial equality and all the other freedoms that had begun to loom large in the 1960s. The new trend began for the Guild when Scottish women's organisations were admitted to the Women's National Commission which advises the Government on all legislation affecting women, and on which many of the major women's organisations in the UK are represented. Elizabeth Anderson, as president of the largest women's organisation in Scotland, was invited to be a commissioner at the annual meeting in London in 1970. There, like every succeeding president of the Guild, she found herself mixing with strange bed-fellows as well as Christians of all denominations, discussing every conceivable subject: like rape, incest, battered wives, single parents, the problems of homelessness, living in hostels, coming out of prison, living on social security—the list was almost endless.

All these issues were taken to Guildswomen through a Communications Group, which was set up in 1971 to ask the branches for their views on all sorts of topics of 'social concern'. This radically altered the look of not a few syllabuses up and down the country, as talks on different aspects of the work of the Church and visits to the Holy Land were interspersed with visits from social workers, Family Planning advisers, Marriage Guidance counsellors, policemen, firemen and experts on drug abuse. Lady Grisell Baillie would surely have had an attack of the vapours at some of the subjects that were discussed over tea in the church hall.

So it was a well-informed and progressive-minded audience that faced the guest speaker at the Annual Meeting in 1972—the most talked-about, the most controversial woman of the time, Mrs Mary Whitehouse, secretary of the National Viewers and Listeners Association, self-appointed guardian of the country's moral standards. Mrs Whitehouse no doubt expected unanimous agreement with her views from this vast audience of committed churchwomen; but in the event, many were less than enamoured with her uncompromising attitude to contraception and abortion, and quite a few were positively incensed at her attack on the Family Planning Association:

> The greatest threat to our society today comes not from the anarchists or the Communists, but from groups like the Family Planning Association, which flourish under the humanist banner. They were the people who were behind the moves for abortion, euthanasia, sex education and the removal of religious education in schools. Their teaching was quite specifically anti-Christ.
>
> (*The Scotsman*)

Angry letters to *The Scotsman* followed, including one from the Guild president herself, Elizabeth Anderson:

> Many of the Woman's Guild members present at our annual meeting last Tuesday regretted Mrs Whitehouse's sweeping attack on the Family Planning Association. I made it quite clear in thanking Mrs Whitehouse from the platform that many of us would not agree with all that she said, but that we were most grateful to her for stimulating discussion which we hoped would continue in the Branches next session.

Discussion certainly did continue in the Branches, and in the Groups, not only on the subject of family planning but on a whole host of social issues on which the Women's National Commission was canvassing opinions. The Guild's Communications Group sent out 'Help' forms to aid Branch discussions; and now, at the time when Mrs Maidie Hart succeeded to the presidency (1972–75), another major issue began to dominate Guild thinking: the highly topical, highly controversial issue of feminism.

Maidie Hart, from Bridge of Weir in Renfrewshire, had arrived at the University of St Andrews in 1939 two years before Elizabeth Anderson. She left with a first class honours degree in English, and a husband who became a research scientist with the Royal Navy. Mrs Hart was a young mother with two little girls by the time she joined the Woman's Guild of Cramond Church, Edinburgh, in 1945; by the time she was appointed national president in 1972, she was a young grandmother.

Like Elizabeth Anderson before her, Maidie Hart was deeply affected by the powerful influences within the Women's National Commission and the World Council of Churches. Her eyes were opened to other worlds. The genteel Edinburgh housewife from a true-blue Conservative background found herself on committees with communists and humanists, women's libbers and nuclear disarmers. She even took part in a Campaign for Nuclear Disarmament (CND) sit-in at the nuclear submarine base at Faslane. Mrs Hart also became part of the powerful feminist movement which swept through the 1970s and found much support among Christian women who felt frustrated by the age-old male dominance of Church affairs. She could point with some pride to the promotion of women to the eldership and to the ministry in the Church of Scotland—the first established Church in Britain to do so. But then she had to admit that six years after their admission to the eldership, women were still outnumbered by 20 to one in the Kirk's highest court, the General Assembly, and were hardly represented at all on Presbyteries; there were still many kirk sessions with no women at all, and only a handful of women held positions of real importance in the Kirk's vast spiritual and social network. In some cases, women were simply not being invited to become elders; in others, the offer was refused. By 1972, women had barely had time to become ministers, apart from a few who were already trained and ready for the Go in 1968. All in all, the 'seelence' was dying hard.

'Feminist', in the full rigour of the word, is not the way to describe Maidie Hart's position. Instead, the 'Community of Women and Men' became the main preoccupation of Maidie Hart's presidency, and she was still working towards this idea—the equal sharing of responsibility between men and women in the Kirk—right up to 1986, when she helped to prepare a report for the Board of World Mission and Unity, calling on the General Assembly to instruct Presbyteries to plan for a fairer representation of women in their membership, and to encourage congregations to appoint more women elders. In particular, it called on the Assembly to urge, and even insist upon, the use, in hymn books and other liturgical material, and in the leading of worship, of what has now become known as 'inclusive language'; this means, for example, saying 'all people' instead of 'mankind', 'children of God' instead of 'sons of God', 'sisters and brothers' instead of 'brethren', and so on. This desire by Christian feminists (with considerable support from men in the Church) to reform the male emphasis in religious language had not yet surfaced during Maidie Hart's time as national president; but it was to cause a minor disturbance in the Guild a few years later.

Mrs Hart's great desire was to 'demythologise' the Woman's Guild —to dispel its aura of exclusiveness and tradition, and bring it down to earth as an effective working force capable of tackling major issues of the day. To this end, for instance, she persuaded the Central Committee to change the traditional time and place of the Annual Meeting. The custom of meeting in the Usher Hall during Assembly Week in May had been started to enable ministers and their wives to go to Edinburgh together; the men to attend the Kirk's highest court, the General Assembly, in the Assembly Hall on the Mound, and the

women to join the throng at the Guild's Annual Meeting in the Usher
Hall. But now that women were beginning to be appointed as Com-
missioners to the General Assembly, they were having to choose
between Assembly and Guild. By changing their annual get-together to
April, the Guild would avoid the conflict of loyalties and also give
themselves the opportunity of using the Assembly Hall as their own
venue. It provided a smaller and more compact forum in which the
Guildswomen could feel more involved and participate better in discussions from the floor than in the vast anonymity of the Usher Hall. There
was another advantage to Mrs Hart's mind: since the General Assembly
was not in session in April, there would be no visitation by the Lord
High Commissioner and his retinue (although the Moderator continued to look in); and since April can be expected to be cold and wet or
windy in Edinburgh, the famous Usher Hall display of summer hats
gave way, perforce, to more workmanlike headgear and gradually to
the general state of hatlessness that pertains today.

The first Annual Meeting in the Assembly Hall was held in April
1973. Not everybody liked it. Many missed the hustle and bustle and
excitement of Edinburgh in Assembly Week. They missed the pomp
and the dressing up. They also found it harder to get a ticket for the
opening-day meeting, because the Assembly Hall, with its capacity of
under 2000, was much smaller than the Usher Hall. But most women
soon settled into the more relaxed yet business-like atmosphere, enjoying the feeling of being close to what was going on; some of them,
indeed, were experiencing for the first time the thrill of speaking at an
Annual Meeting.

Maidie Hart promised even more change in her 1973 Report to the
General Assembly:

> The Woman's Guild recognises that many factors are combining today to
> change its traditional role in the life of the Church.
>   The Woman's Guild believes that this must include . . . a willingness,
> along with other organisations, to *submerge its separate identity* in the wider
> role and responsibilities of the Church family, as the caring community
> in the local situation.

The logic of it led Maidie Hart to only one, inexorable conclusion:

> This could mean that at some point in the future the Woman's Guild, as
> such, might have to phase out, or find a quite different role.

It was an alarming thought, both for the great mass of Guildswomen
who were perfectly content with the Guild as it was, and for ministers
and congregations so dependent on the fund-raising efforts of their

Guild that existence without the Guild was practically inconceivable. Perhaps it was this fear that encouraged the Fathers and Brethren of the General Assembly in 1974 to do something that the Guild had asked for away back in 1932—to elect the Guild national president a 'corresponding member' of the Assembly with the right to speak to her own Reports. Mrs Hart did not, however, win the right to vote in the Assembly.

As president of the only Scottish organisation represented on the Women's National Commission, Maidie Hart was in charge of the plans to celebrate International Women's Year in Scotland in 1975. She rallied various other women's organisations as well as the Woman's Guild, and the result was a great jamboree at Edinburgh Castle, with women from every walk of life displaying their aims and achievements on behalf of the community and the world; and it seemed quite natural, now, to find the Communist Women's stand situated in friendly camaraderie between the Woman's Guild and the Mothers' Union.

Before the end of her presidency, Maidie Hart went to Nairobi as the Guild delegate to the World Council of Churches; when her term was over, she and the Revd Bill Johnstone (who had been a fellow delegate) made up a roadshow of slides, tapes and music illustrating the theme of the Nairobi conference, *Jesus Christ Frees and Unites*, and took it around churches, Guilds, schools and halls from the Borders to Orkney—200 meetings in two years. In 1977 she founded the Scottish Convention of Women. She became an elder of Cramond Church. She visited China, and went to the USSR as a guest of the Soviet Women's Committee, whose chairwoman, astronaut Valentina Cherewska, she had met at a Woman of the Year lunch. Immediately afterwards, Maidie Hart went round the Guild Branches, giving talks about China and Soviet Russia: the long age of 'seelence' among women in the Kirk was well and truly over.

But despite the indefatigable vigour and intellectual drive of Maidie Hart's presidency, there was nothing, it seemed, that could halt the remorseless decline in the membership numbers of the Woman's Guild. In 1972, the total had dropped below 100 000 for the first time since 1933; by 1975 it was down to 82 489—barely more than half of that triumphant peak of 160 000 only two decades earlier.

16

Self-examination

Mrs Mary Millican (1975–78) seemed predestined to lead the largest organisation of women in Scotland one day; from the day she left school in Inverness, every path seemed to lead to the national presidency of the Woman's Guild. As Mary MacLean, whose mother was a Guildswoman and father an elder of the Kirk, she joined the East Church branch of the Girls' Association, and then went on to work as the GA's national secretary at its headquarters at 121 George Street. There she became steeped in all the intricacies of Church government, the courts and committees, the departments and boards; she knew the system from top to bottom. She knew the conveners and secretaries, ministers and deaconesses, and everything about the administration of women's work in the Church. As secretary of the Girls' Association she was made an associate member of the Guild Central Committee in 1947.

After marrying a farmer in Berwickshire, Mary Millican joined her local branch of the Guild, and on the birth of her first child, became a member of the Young Mothers' Group. With her tremendous experience of Guild work, her expertise at running committees and her general ability and air of competence, she soon sped to the top of the Guild pyramid; but she waited until her third child was out of primary school before accepting the full-time, unpaid, round-the-clock, exhausting and totally demanding job of national president in 1975.

Her experience was tremendously varied. She had been editor of *Compass*, the magazine of the Women's Home Mission Committee, and the first editor of the Guild magazine *Spotlight* in 1968. She was a member of a committee set up by the General Assembly in 1973 to study the question of Parapsychology; and in 1974 she was the Guild representative who went to Berlin for the World Council of Churches' consultation on 'Sexism in the Seventies'. She might have been expected to return from that experience as a tub-thumping women's liberationist; instead, as she wrote in. *Spotlight*, larger issues prevailed:

> As the Consultation progressed we discovered . . . that the liberation of
> women cannot be separated from other forms of discrimination and
> oppression, but must be viewed in the context of the struggle for a more
> open future . . . free from every form of injustice—from racism, sexism,
> social and economic oppression and cultural domination.

Her favourite quotation on the subject of sexism came from a delegate
from Sri Lanka:

> In Sri Lanka, as in most countries of the Third World, the problem is not
> whether the wife has spent too many hours in the kitchen cooking, but
> whether she has any food at all to cook.

So instead of feminism, world hunger became Mary Millican's
overriding concern. The Central Committee held a special seminar,
addressed by an expert on world hunger, and drew up a list of
suggestions to help Guildswomen 'to explore the facts and stimulate
them to action'. The list was sent to every branch and group. It ranged
from the titles of relevant periodicals and newspapers to suggestions as
to how each Guildswoman could take personal action—for instance, by
observing such precepts as: 'Never waste food', 'Eat for fitness', 'Avoid
over-packaging', 'Live simply that others may simply live'.

The Central Committee showed the way by instituting a 'Be My
Guest' scheme, whereby members agreed to set aside, once a week,
what it would cost to entertain a guest to a meal. The money was
collected a year later and donated to Christian Aid, and Mary Millican
called on Presbyterial councils, branches and groups to start similar
schemes. 'Hunger Lunches' and £1-a-head meals of dry bread and water
were laid before congregations in church halls throughout the land, and
branch meetings were regaled with facts about drought, disease,
agricultural methods and average rainfalls, as well as the advantages
of a high-fibre diet, free-range eggs, organic vegetables and recycled
envelopes.

Just as the early Guild had balanced its efforts in the foreign field with
care for the needy at home, so Mary Millican's leadership also focussed
on deprivation and homelessness in our own country. 'Help' forms
were sent out, encouraging members 'to become informed about the
needs of the single homeless and of one-parent families, and to give
practical help to refuges for battered wives and to city night shelters'.

In her Reports to the General Assembly, Mary Millican sought to
reassure the men who feared the increasing participation of women in
Church government:

I want to say quite emphatically that women are not seeking to replace men in the structures of the Church. What we look forward to is a responsible partnership built on mutual trust and respect, a partnership in which men and women accept their complementary roles, for we believe that both have a distinctive understanding of Christian faith and life and gifts to offer.

She was also careful to reassure the women who feared that the Guild might be phased out eventually, as Maidie Hart had presaged. At the Guild's 90th anniversary in 1977, with the Queen listening from the Throne Gallery of the Assembly Hall, Mary Millican told the General Assembly that the Guild had been reviewing its whole aim and purpose and even whether there was still a place for an all-woman organisation in the Church today:

The radically altered place of women in today's society has compelled us to make a thorough examination of our own situation. We've had to ask some searching questions about the place of the Guild in our Church which, theoretically, offers equal opportunities to men and women. We do not depart from our firmly held belief that the Church operates at its best when it makes the maximum use of the complementary understandings and gifts of men and women, but . . . it's our considered judgement that there is a defensible argument for the continuance of the Woman's Guild.

Indeed, the result of our reflection and assessment is a renewed confidence in the worth of the Guild, and the conviction that, for the foreseeable future, *it is in the interests both of the women of the Church, and of the Church itself, that we should continue.*

This renewed 'reflection and assessment' was the result of a Working Group that Mary Millican had set up to examine afresh the role and function of the Woman's Guild in the face of declining membership and competitive claims on the time and interests of women. One practical outcome was an extension of the 'Teach-Ins' that had been previously instituted: training courses for Guild leaders and office-bearers at Carberry Tower, the Kirk's teaching and conference centre near Musselburgh. They were now to include members from the Young Woman's Group as well; and they proved overwhelmingly popular.

In her final address to the General Assembly, Mary Millican declared:

I reaffirm my confidence in the contribution which the Guild can continue to make to the life and work of the Church, if it is willing to adapt to changing needs and circumstances.

Her own particular contribution had been to widen the Guild's horizons, but also to reinforce the Guild's role as a platform for lively and informed discussion on domestic issues like the standards of television programmes and the provision of religious education in schools. She herself had attended the centennial of the World Alliance of Reformed Churches in St Andrews, the triennial meeting of the United Presbyterian Women in the United States, the centenary of the Scots Kirk in Lausanne, a seminar on the European Economic Community in Luxembourg, and the Women's National Commission in Israel.

In the midst of all this, she had somehow managed to see two daughters graduate, and organise the wedding of the elder, Ishbel, a doctor, who left Scotland in 1986 with her husband and two children to serve as a missionary in Africa.

It can hardly be said that Mrs Mary Millican 'retired' after her presidency was over. An elder in Ayton Church in Berwickshire and a Presbytery elder of Duns, she presently represents the Presbytery on the committee which nominates the Moderator of the General Assembly. She is chairman of the advisory committee on *Life and Work*; and a member of the Executive Committee of the Kirk's publishing house, The Saint Andrew Press. She is also a Governor of the Esdaile Trust (which assists the education and advancement of daughters of ministers, missionaries and widowed deaconesses of the Church of Scotland), and vice-convener of the powerful Church and Nation Committee. She was also a member of the Assembly Council; a member of the Kirk's Publications Committee; and a member of the General Assembly's Special Committee on Communism and Political and Religious Liberty. In her spare time, she was a member of the Children's Panel for Berwickshire, the Scottish Education Committee on Secondary Education, and various Scottish committees for the International Year of Women, the Child, and the Disabled. She was also chairperson of the Scottish Advisory Group of UNICEF (United Nations Children's Fund) from 1979–83, and at present is a member of the Borders Health Board.

As president of the Guild, Mary Millican was a prime example of the indefatigable Guild superwoman, and of the leadership's aim to have Guildswomen applying their talents and Christian influence in as many fields of service as possible. She added another rich thread to the glowing tapestry of charismatic leaders, the long line of women of immense vitality and variety stretching down the years from the indomitable Mrs Charteris.

The next in line was Mrs Daphne MacNab (1978–81), born in England at Mount Seton, near Whitley Bay, to Scots parents from Angus. She was yet another president who had been educated at the University of St Andrews. Daphne MacNab (née McDonald) went there in 1934, took an honours degree in Economics and History, and married a fellow-student, Hamish MacNab. When he came back from the war he trained for the ministry, took up his first charge at Kilrenny, near Anstruther in Fife, in 1948, and never left it. Daphne MacNab, who had grown up blissfully unaware of the existence of such a thing as a Woman's Guild (she was a member of the Presbyterian Church in England), soon found herself president of Kilrenny while bringing up a family of five children (four of whom were to become doctors). She became an elder, and served on the Kirk's Advisory Board, the celebrated 'Committee of Forty', and the Deaconess Board; she was convener of St Colm's Board, and served as vice-convener of the Home Board at the same time as she was a national vice-president of the Guild.

So it was a woman of maturity, with all the experience and confidence of a long reign as the lady of the manse, as the matriarch of a large family, and as a leader in the affairs of the Church and Guild, who became national president in 1978. Perhaps her silver hairs might have fooled some of her younger colleagues into thinking that they had inherited a gentle, old-fashioned motherly type who would sit back and let them get on with things. In fact, as the official Guild tribute to Daphne MacNab put it at the end of her presidency, she was 'an exacting and refreshing colleague'—which was a polite way of saying that Mrs MacNab stood no nonsense from anybody. You don't bring up four doctors and a computer tycoon, run the same manse for 30 years, and do battle with half a dozen important Kirk committees, without acquiring a little bit of authority!

As with every good old-fashioned mother, however, Daphne Mac-Nab's firmness was always tempered by patience and understanding: as the Guild tribute put it, she 'always had time to stop and listen with patience and understanding to any Guild member wishing to share a problem; more often than not she has provided the help, and always the encouragement, that was needed'.

Indeed, it was what she called 'human relationships' within the Guild that was the main preoccupation of Daphne MacNab's presidency. She felt that there was little use in exhorting Guildswomen to go out and take their place in the new world until they had re-appraised their whole attitude to life, analysed their motives, sorted themselves out as individuals. She re-planned the training courses at Carberry to provide 'formation training', first for leaders and then for any members of branch or group.

'What kind of people are we?' they asked themselves at these sessions. 'What kind of people might we become as we exercise, thoughtfully and prayerfully, the choices open to us?' 'What kind of branch and group do we need to allow women to develop the gifts specially right for today, and to support them in the new roles being assumed?'

Deaconess Jean Grigor (later Mrs Bill Morrison) was in charge of these self-analysing group sessions, using her expertise as Group Relations Adviser of the Kirk's Department of Education. Bible study and worship were 'integral parts of the formative process', and Communion was celebrated after breakfast in the dining-room each morning. Ultra-committed types could sign on for an advanced course in 'deepening personal relationships'.

With hindsight it might all seem to smack of the psycho-analytical, bare-your-soul, who-am-I, social introspection that became so fashionable in the 1970s. But the courses were immensely popular—so much so that it was decided to take them to Guildswomen who could not manage to get to Carberry. The first extra-mural course was held in Dingwall in 1980. Later, Daphne MacNab took her training team to Lewis, Kirkcudbright, Wigtown, Lanark, Dumfries, Buchan, Gordon and down to Corby in England.

The President's Group, too, had a training session—'to encourage the personal and corporate spiritual growth of this non executive group which acts as a "think-tank" for the Guild'. The Central Executive had a day-course at St Colm's, and the Central Committee were given a sample course, too, so that they could recommend it to their councils and branches. In the words of the 1980 Annual Report:

> We believe that this is the area in which we may come to discern the next step forward for the Guild as an organisation.

In the following year's Report, Daphne MacNab reaffirmed and expanded the underlying philosophy behind the scheme:

> The deepening of relationships and the seeking of closer and more supportive acceptance of each other in Christian commitment has brought new insights. Sharing together, we have come to perceive that the theological question today is not so much what we say or do, but rather how we relate to each other. . . .
>
> Urged on by mounting evidence that the world is too small for anything but love, we have sought to experience the Guild as a corporate body in which gifts and resources are pooled for the benefit of all people. . . .
>
> We are beginning to appreciate what it means to accept that mission is not confined to the personal and spiritual dimensions but includes . . . a responsibility to seek justice and peace in the world.

What did all this introspection mean to the ordinary Guildswoman sitting in her favourite seat by the radiator at the local Guild meeting?

Not a great deal, perhaps. But Daphne MacNab had also declared her belief in that much-maligned institution, the regular branch meeting, in earlier Reports:

> The Branch and Group meeting, for many members, remains the focal point of the Guild. At it, members participate in worship that is imaginative, intimate and meaningful. The fellowship enjoyed is more than a friendly acquaintance; it is supportive and caring, arising from a genuine concern for each and every member. (1978)
>   The real life of the Guild takes place at the local meeting. (1979)

Taken together, she was reminding the women in the parishes that the whole world was their concern, and that they could do their bit right on their own doorstep. She summed it up with her ringing slogan: 'Act Locally and Think Globally'.

And in the best traditions of the Guild, old age was honoured as much as youth was encouraged. During Mrs MacNab's presidency, a new branch of the Woman's Guild was opened—in one of the Kirk's Eventide Homes. Queen Mary House Woman's Guild, in Crosshill, Glasgow, meets once a fortnight; its programmes are strong on films, slide-shows and musical entertainments, but correspondingly short on visiting speakers, since many of its members are so hard of hearing. The executive is drawn from half a dozen local Guilds, who act as the eyes and ears and legs of the elderly members; but three of the oldest residents have attended delegate meetings in Edinburgh. Mrs Winifred Blyth, for 30 years a delegate for Greenhill Parish Church, Rutherglen, went as the Queen Mary House delegate to the Social Responsibility annual meeting when she was 89 years old, and almost totally blind; when she came back she gave a crisp and accurate account of the proceedings, without a single note. Mrs Marjorie McWalter, once president of Giffnock South Guild, knit 20 self-designed baby suits in 10 months for the Guild's Ethiopian effort in 1985.

When Daphne MacNab retired as national president in 1981, the official Guild tribute summed up her main achievement for posterity:

> Mrs MacNab . . . has encouraged Guildswomen to develop confidence in using their gifts, and a growing willingness to undertake new ways of working in the Guild.

It also expressed 'the feeling that the Woman's Guild will never be the same again'. This was meant as a sincere tribute to the changes she had brought about during her presidency; but in the light of later events, it can be read as an uncannily prophetic intimation of things to come. For the next president of the Woman's Guild was to be a woman called Mrs Anne Hepburn.

17

God Our Mother!

On the opening day of the Annual Meeting in April, 1982, the national president, Mrs Anne Hepburn (1981–84), uttered a prayer the like of which had never been heard in the Church of Scotland, far less the Woman's Guild:

> God our Mother, you give birth to all life, and love us to the uttermost. Your love surrounds and feeds us. Within your love we find our home, our joy, our freedom. You open the world to us and give us room to change and grow.
>
> As you love us, so you love all your children. Help us, dear Mother God, to catch something of your love: your delight in others' uniqueness, your grief at their suffering, your patience and forgiveness, your passion for reconciliation and peace throughout the world.
>
> We thank you, our God, that we have come to another Annual Meeting and we ask you to bless us in all that we do today; that this meeting may be for each of us an opportunity to grow in the grace and knowledge of our Lord and Saviour, Jesus Christ.
>
> To whom be the glory both now and for ever. Amen.

And with these quiet words—a prayer composed by a United Reformed Church minister, Brian Wren, and published by Christian Aid—Anne Hepburn set off a controversy that would make the Woman's Guild the focus of world-wide attention.

Anne Hepburn (née Burton) was born and brought up in the South Ayrshire village of Dailly, where her father was an elder in the Kirk. She graduated at the University of Glasgow and came back to Ayrshire to teach in a rural school at Barr, before deciding to become a missionary. She trained at St Colm's in Edinburgh and was sent to Nyasaland (now Malawi) in 1950 as a teacher at the Girls' School in Blantyre. There she married a colleague, the Revd James L Hepburn, and they served together until 1966 in the Church of Central Africa Presbyterian at Mlanje and Zomba.

When the Hepburns returned to Scotland with a young family of three children, Anne was disappointed at what she felt was the inertia and apathy of churchwomen in Scotland compared with those in Africa. She herself was small and energetic, only five feet two inches tall, a wee pocket dynamo, her eyes sparkling behind large spectacles, her straight black fringe of hair bobbing restlessly. She quickly made her mark in the Guild, and by 1973 had become a national vice-president.

In 1975—what she called her 'watershed year'—she made her first appearance as a Commissioner to the General Assembly, as an elder of St Mary's, Kirkcudbright. At the Assembly, her contributions to debate left the Fathers and Brethren in no doubt that she was 'one of them'—a Christian feminist, and probably the deadliest of the species because of her obvious sincerity and deeply religious motivation. But her conciseness and straightforward style won her many friends and opened many doors, and she found herself moving effortlessly into the corridors of Kirk power as a member of the Assembly Council.

By the time Anne Hepburn became national president of the Guild in 1981 she was a kenspeckle figure, liked for her cheery extrovert nature and renowned as a speaker with the tenacity of a terrier in debate—but also for having a 'bee in her bunnet' about women's rights. It was the Year of the Orange Boycott, and Anne Hepburn (not surprisingly in the light of her experiences in Africa and on the Inter-Church Relations Committee) masterminded a Woman's Guild campaign to boycott South African goods, especially oranges, as a protest against apartheid.

But it was the famous, or infamous (depending on your point of view) 'God the Mother' prayer on the opening day of the 1982 Annual Meeting that really pitchforked Anne Hepburn, and the Woman's Guild, into the harsh glare of sensational publicity.

People who were there on that day said that a hissing sound was heard in the hall, like a mass intake of breath. Anne Hepburn herself said afterwards that she had not noticed any undue reaction, and had not intended to provoke one:

> I felt it was right to use the prayer that day. I wasn't trying to prove anything, or start up anything. I know it sounds pious, but I felt moved by the Holy Spirit.

Intentional or not, however, she must have been aware that there were many in the Guild who would object strongly to hearing God addressed as 'Mother'. This was the ultimate in 'inclusive language', with a vengeance, and was bound to offend those who look on any deviation from the exact words of the Bible as heresy.

Curiously enough, there was no Press reaction at first. No one had alerted them in advance. There was a certain amount of tut-tutting in the tea-shops of the High Street, but only two letters of complaint were received at the Guild headquarters at 121 George Street. And there the matter might well have ended, as a tiny tremor rather than an earth-quake, had it not been for the events at the General Assembly a month later. On 19 May 1982, Anne Hepburn went to the microphone to present the Annual Report of the Woman's Guild. Here was no firebrand oratory. There was no mention of *that* Prayer. Her theme, reasoned and unimpassioned, was about the Church's need to make fuller use of the spiritual gifts and practical energies of the women of the Church. Only one sentence in it hinted at the real direction of her thoughts:

> How hard it is to address and envisage God in ways that respect the Christian understanding of personhood rather than suggest male super-iority.

One man who had been present at the opening day of the Annual Meeting and had heard *that* Prayer was the Revd James I. Weatherhead, convener of the Business Committee. Now he stood up and surprised everyone—including Anne Hepburn—by putting the following proposal:

> To invite the Woman's Guild to appoint a small study group to consult with the Panel on Doctrine on the theological implications of the motherhood of God, and report to a subsequent General Assembly.

It was not, he assured the Moderator, a frivolous motion. Anne Hepburn, hardly able to believe her good fortune at having such an offer out of the blue from the Assembly, quickly assented:

> Moderator, I wholeheartedly accept this deliverance from Mr Weather-head. I would welcome it very much, and I think the time is overdue for such a study group to consult with the Panel on Doctrine. I welcome it, Mr Moderator.

After earnest debate, the General Assembly passed Mr Weather-head's proposal by 390 votes to 290.

Next morning *The Scotsman* declared:

> By persuading the General Assembly to study the concept of the mother-hood of God, the Woman's Guild pulled off a feminist coup yesterday.

Anne Hepburn did not like that at all. The Guild, she claimed, had not persuaded anyone to do anything, and she had been as surprised as anyone, both at the proposal and its acceptance by the Assembly. But despite the jibe about the 'feminist coup', *The Scotsman* approved of it:

> The Woman's Guild have opened up an intriguing question, one of considerable difficulty and delicacy. Yet they are entirely right to question established verbal usages. . . . The language of worship does enshrine a paternalist attitude which requires thorough scrutiny.

Yet by and large the members of the Woman's Guild were reluctant to provide that thorough scrutiny. There was little response to the president's invitation in her annual letter to branch presidents in September 1982, for contributions to the Study Group from local groups; few Guilds, if any, seemed to have bothered to discuss the matter.

The joint Study Group set up to examine the question and report to the General Assembly consisted of ten people, six appointed by the Woman's Guild and four by the Panel on Doctrine—seven women and three men—of whom four were ministers:

From the Woman's Guild:
Mrs Anne Hepburn (convener: Guild national president)
Mrs Ann Allen (president of Chryston Woman's Guild)
Mrs Dorothy Dalgliesh (former Guild national vice-president
Mrs Clara Macrae (former Guild Central Executive member)
Mrs Daphne MacNab (former Guild national president)
Mrs Jean Morrison (former Group Relations Adviser)

From the Panel on Doctrine
The Revd John C L Gibson (Hebrew & Old Testament Studies, New College)
The Revd Sheilagh Kesting (parish minister of Overton, Wishaw)
The Revd Dr Alan E Lewis (Report editor: secretary of the Panel)
The Revd Dr Ian McIntosh (parish minister of Old High, Inverness)

The Report, which was published in April, 1984, was a majority report. The conclusion of the majority was that Scripture provides precedents for 'the restrained and sensitive use of feminine language both to describe and address God'. The minority, however, felt that although there are some feminine analogies for God in the Bible, to call God 'Mother' would be illegitimate and would cause pain. The majority were more concerned about the pain of 'those who feel alienated and distanced from God by the exclusive use of male language for God'. The Report called on the Church to take this particular pain more seriously:

> for they believe that they have heard it said in the Word of God that the Father of our Lord Jesus Christ, the Maker of us all, resembles, though he

far transcends, everything that is best in the female way of being human
and the human way of being motherly.

The Kirk's publishers, The Saint Andrew Press, published the
Report as a paperback special entitled *The Motherhood of God* in time for
the 1984 Annual Meeting of the Woman's Guild. Anne Hepburn,
knowing that many Guildswomen had complained that the whole issue
had been foisted on them without prior consultation, invited Dr Alan
Lewis, the editor of the Report, to talk about it on the opening day. It
turned out to be a catastrophic mistake. For the first time in the history
of the Guild, a guest speaker was actually hissed and booed. Next
morning the newspapers were in full cry. Suddenly the Woman's Guild
had gained notoriety. The more tabloid the paper, the more ungodly its
normal preoccupations, the more indignantly it castigated the
Woman's Guild. 'OUR MOTHER WHICH ART IN HEAVEN,'
screamed the *Daily Star* headline. 'It is the kind of stuff that gets both
religion and women a bad name,' wrote one journalist. Another
columnist—a woman—sneered, 'If Jesus had been a woman she
wouldn't have joined the Woman's Guild'.

The letter columns of *The Scotsman* fumed with indignation. One
man said he was leaving the Church of Scotland immediately. A
woman wrote, 'The hand that has rocked the cradle is now rocking the
boat'. A minister wrote: 'God (dare I say He) must be heartily scun-
nered by now of the "monstrous regiment of women" bent on making
Him, at least, a eunuch'.

One Guildswoman, Elspeth Dale from Kilmarnock, replied that 'the
monstrous regiment' of women was most unhappy about the time
being wasted by its generals on 'this trifling subject'. And that seems to
have been the overwhelming view of Guild members. The only speaker
who had been thunderously applauded on that disastrous opening day
of the Annual Meeting was a local Guild president, Mary Philip, of
Holyrood Abbey, who had deplored the fact that so much time had
been spent on the Motherhood of God issue at a time of crisis and moral
and spiritual decline.

When the 'Motherhood of God' Report was presented to the General
Assembly on 22 May, as part of the annual Guild Report, the Fathers
and Brethren gave it short shrift. Its contents were not even discussed.
Instead, Anne Hepburn was subjected to an unpleasant inquisition, as if
she were in the dock, and her replies were interrupted by foot-tapping,
tut-tutting, heckling—or else received in stony silence. A divinity
student writing to *The Scotsman* called it 'one of the most appallingly
ungracious and narrow-minded displays of masculine paranoia I have

ever witnessed'. The General Assembly voted merely to thank the Study Group for the Report and depart from it *simpliciter*—in other words, to dismiss it without debate.

Next day the newspapers carried reports of women crying in the corridors of the Assembly Hall. There was a spate of headlines, ranging from the *San Francisco Examiner's* 'Presbyterians turn down a female God' to the *Scottish Daily Record's* 'Our Father which art in Heaven is no Mother'. Anne Hepburn herself was described as 'a monstrous regiment of women all on her own—no female has caused such a disruption in the Kirk since Jenny Geddes'—and as 'the woman who put "her" into heresy'.

The issue was taken up and given a thorough airing in the media in France and Australia, America and Ireland, in newspapers, radio and television, on chat shows and current affairs programmes. The Saint Andrew Press was kept busy supplying the great demand for copies of the paperback. Much of the coverage was more sensational than sensible; but serious interest in the implications of the issue has never really died away.

Newspaper claims that the Motherhood of God issue had 'split the Woman's Guild' were woefully inaccurate. The vast majority of Guildswomen hardly knew what all the fuss was about, and cared even less. They had other and, to them, more important things to think about. For one thing, there was a new national president in office—Mrs May Smith (1984–87); and when Mrs Smith presided the following year at her first Annual Meeting, the atmosphere was the same as ever—busy, bubbling, warm and enthusiastic.

May Smith had climbed the pyramid from the Young Mothers' Fellowship of St Philip's, Joppa—she had been the first Young Mother to be co-opted on to the Guild's Central Committee. She was vice-convener of the Kirk's Board of Social Responsibility, convener of the housekeeping and staff committee of Carberry Tower, and a member of the Board of Education. Now a grandmother, with a quiet sense of humour and a calm, unruffled approach to life, May Smith slipped easily into the exacting post of president, and was able to report to the General Assembly in 1986 that the Woman's Guild was going from strength to strength, in local communities, in churches and presbyteries, on national boards and ecumenical councils. Admittedly, membership was down to 77 418 (including 10 000 members of Young Woman's Groups), but total giving for the year had risen to £868 363—a magnificent achievement.

May Smith asked the Assembly to designate Sunday, 26 April 1987 as 'Woman's Guild Sunday', for the centenary year only, to celebrate 'the organisation which has evolved and adapted to the changes and upheavals of a turbulent century, while still striving to remain true to the vision of its founder, Dr Archibald Charteris'. The Annual Meeting heard that public parks all over Scotland would have floral displays in red, white, blue and gold—the colours of the Guild badge—to celebrate the centenary, and Guildswomen were invited to plant their own gardens in the Guild colours. There were also hopes that British Rail might name one of its engines 'Woman's Guild'. And in addition to a souvenir scarf (already selling well), a pendant (available in silver and base metal), a pen, a 'one-off' commemorative tin of Cadbury's chocolate biscuits (produced as a goodwill gesture by the manufacturers), and a selection of Scriptures (produced in association with the National Bible Society), a commemorative pictorial brochure will also be available, sponsored substantially by a Bank (and one or two other major concerns). A wall-hanging to mark the Centenary will be a specially designed major piece of embroidery and appliqué destined for the foyer of 121 George Street. Many more items and occasions are being considered, including a pageant of the Guild's history at the 1987 Annual Meeting.

As the Guildswomen packing the Assembly Hall at the 1986 meeting warmed to the news of the centenary plans; as they began to plan their own local celebrations and branch histories; as they raised the roof with their splendid hymn-singing; as former national presidents beamed happily in their special seats in the gallery—Isabel Douglas, Elizabeth Anderson, Maidie Hart, Mary Millican, Daphne MacNab, Anne Hepburn, and dear Jessie Dingwall—it was impossible to imagine that this great family of women would ever come to an end. Fashions may change, women may take their place as full partners with men in the courts of the Church, and some may deem a separate organisation for women to be no longer necessary; but May Smith entertained no doubts. As she wrote in the Annual Report:

> The Guild is grasping this opportunity to give thanks for the past and also *to examine its role in its second century.*

It is the sort of optimism that would have gladdened the heart of Dr Archibald Hamilton Charteris; the man who worked to bring the women of the Church of Scotland 'out of silence'.

Index